LOST RA
OF
SUSSEX

Other Railways titles available from Countryside Books include:

Cheshire Railways Remembered

Lost Railways of the Chilterns

Lost Railways of Dorset

Lost Railways of East Anglia

Lost Railways of Hampshire

LOST RAILWAYS OF SUSSEX

Leslie Oppitz

COUNTRYSIDE BOOKS
NEWBURY, BERKSHIRE

First published 2001

Reprinted 2002, 2005

COUNTRYSIDE BOOKS
3 Catherine Road
Newbury, Berkshire

To view our complete range of books,
please visit us at
www.countrysidebooks.co.uk

ISBN 1 85306 697 4

The cover picture shows a Q class 0-6-0 approaching East Grinstead
High Level from Oxted on 22nd May 1948.
(from an original painting by Colin Doggett)
Maps by Jennie Collins

Produced through MRM Associates Ltd., Reading
Printed by Woolnough Bookbinding Ltd., Irthlingborough

CONTENTS

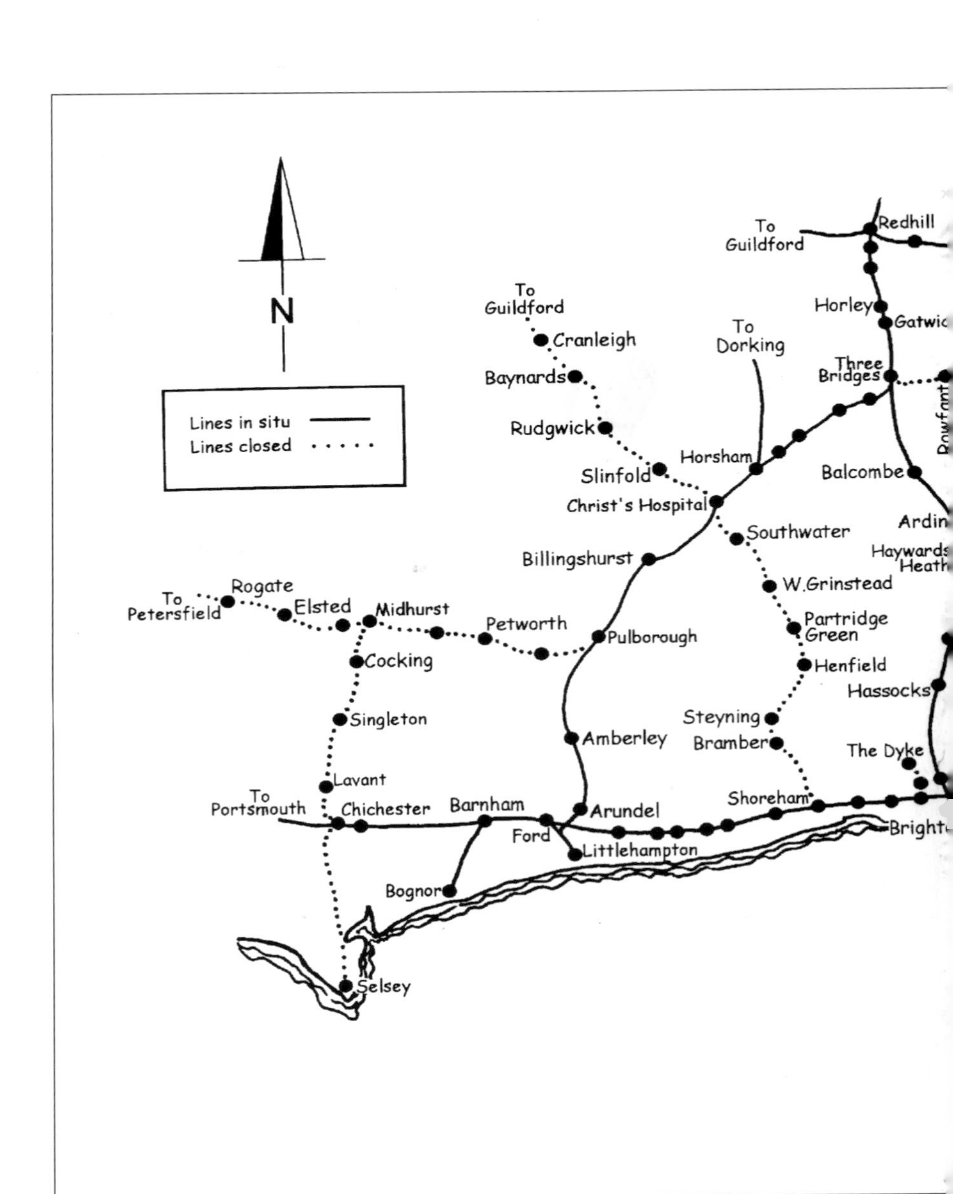

N
Lines in situ
Lines closed
To Guildford
Redhill
Horley
Gatwic
To Guildford
Cranleigh
Baynards
Rudgwick
Slinfold
To Dorking
Horsham
Three Bridges
Balcombe
Christ's Hospital
Southwater
Ardin
Haywards Heath
Billingshurst
W.Grinstead
Partridge Green
Henfield
Hassocks
Rogate
To Petersfield
Elsted
Midhurst
Petworth
Pulborough
Cocking
Singleton
Steyning
Bramber
Amberley
The Dyke
Lavant
To Portsmouth
Chichester
Barnham
Arundel
Shoreham
Ford
Littlehampton
Bright
Bognor
Selsey

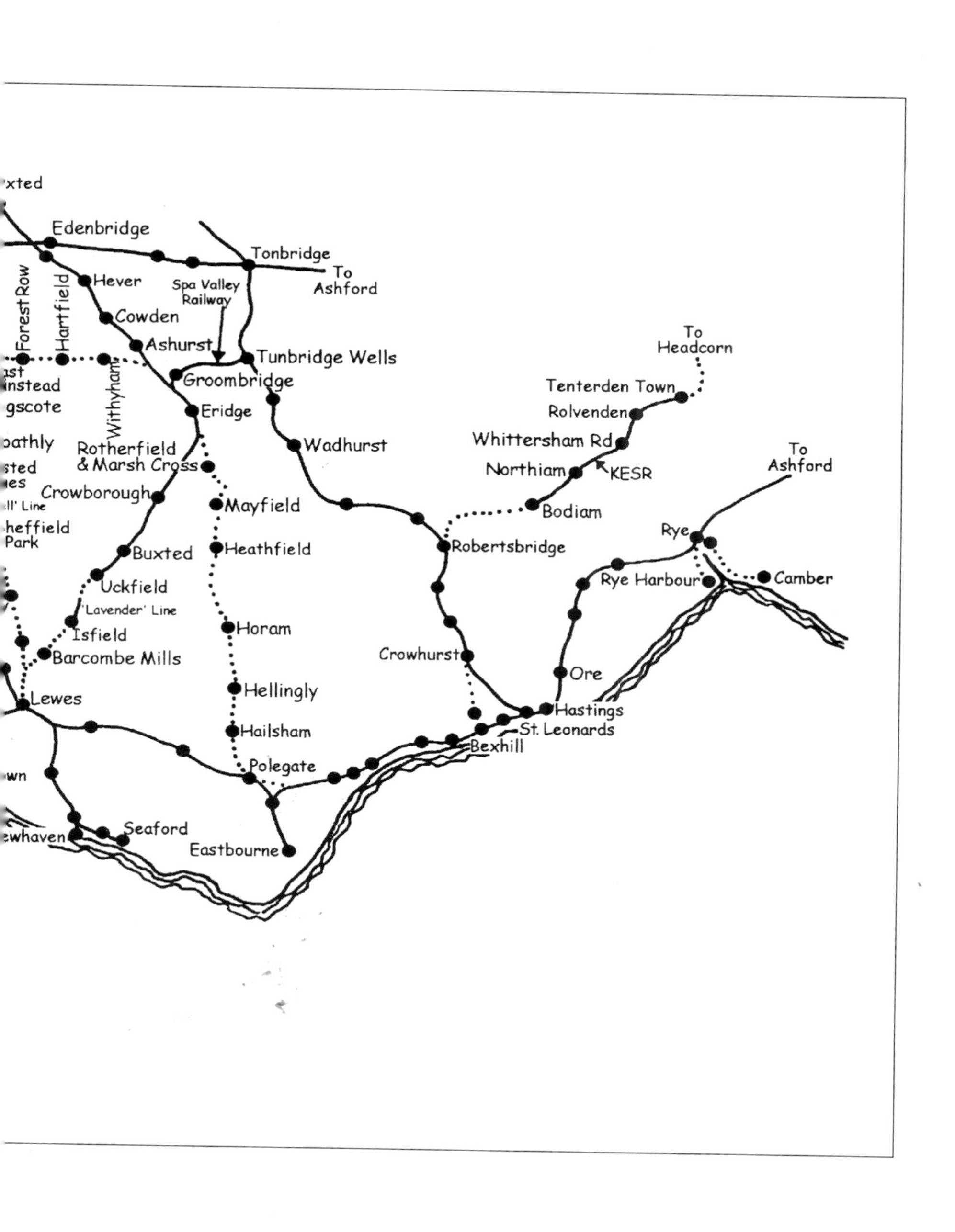

Edenbridge
Tonbridge
To Ashford
Hever
Spa Valley Railway
Cowden
Forest Row
Hartfield
Ashurst
Tunbridge Wells
Groombridge
Withyham
Eridge
Rotherfield & Marsh Cross
Wadhurst
Crowborough
Mayfield
Buxted
Heathfield
Uckfield
'Lavender' Line
Isfield
Barcombe Mills
Horam
Hellingly
Lewes
Hailsham
Polegate
Seaford
Eastbourne
To Headcorn
Tenterden Town
Rolvenden
Whittersham Rd
Northiam
KESR
Bodiam
Robertsbridge
To Ashford
Rye
Rye Harbour
Camber
Crowhurst
Ore
Hastings
St. Leonards
Bexhill

ABBREVIATIONS

The following abbreviations are used in this book:

BR	British Rail
DEMU	Diesel Electric Multiple Unit
GWR	Great Western Railway
KESR	Kent & East Sussex Railway
LBSCR	London, Brighton & South Coast Railway
LCDR	London, Chatham & Dover Railway
LCGB	Locomotive Club of Great Britain
LMS	London, Midland & Scottish Railway
LNER	London & North Eastern Railway
LSWR	London & South Western Railway
RCTS	Railway Correspondence & Travel Society
SECR	South Eastern & Chatham Railway
SER	South Eastern Railway
SHDR	Shoreham, Horsham & Dorking Railway
SR	Southern Railway

Please note:

'Junction' implies a railway station
'junction' means where railway lines meet.

ACKNOWLEDGEMENTS

Acknowledgements are due to the many libraries and record offices throughout Sussex where staff have delved into records, and to the late John Smith of Lens of Sutton for his help in supplying many early pictures. Thanks also go to John H. Meredith and Rod K. Blencowe for their pictures. I am grateful to Bill Trite, Chairman of the Swanage Railway Company Ltd, for his help given by identifying many early locomotives and Colin Doggett for his splendid cover picture. The following also made valuable contributions:

Arthur Tayler, C. Eng F. I. Mech. E., of Betchworth, Surrey
J. E. Potter, Secretary to the Board, Bluebell Railway PLC
Mrs Sandra Marsh, Marketing Executive, Kent & East Sussex Railway
Rod Peters of the Lavender Line, Isfield
Peter Lawne of Spa Valley Railway, Tunbridge Wells
Sally Parsons, Librarian, Information Services, Wealden Group
Mary-Lou Rapley of The Old Railway Station at Petworth
Tony Johnson of Chichester
Norbet Gutowski of Old Station House, Singleton.

Personal thanks go to Doreen Judge who typed my original 1987 manuscript, also Desmond Adams and Nigel Oppitz for their help. Finally, thanks to my wife, Joan, who toured Sussex with me, also for her patience and help in preparing and checking the manuscript.

Introduction

All too frequently today the words 'dismantled railway' can be seen on an up-to-date Ordnance Survey map. Possibly the route can be walked and, on following the course, remnants from an earlier railway line can be found. Where an overgrown track may now exist, busy locomotives once made their way across the countryside pulling coaches filled with people and linking remote towns and villages.

At the start of the 19th century no conventional railways existed in Sussex. Passenger travel and movement of freight was by road, canal or by coastal vessels. In Sussex one of the first turnpikes was a trust established in 1696 covering a road from Crawley to Reigate in Surrey. More were to follow and by 1770 a turnpike was established from London to Brighton. Canals were dug in the early 1800s adding to the numerous rivers already made navigable but such transport was slow and none of these ventures was financially successful.

In 1809 the first form of railway came to Sussex. Built close to the Chalk Pit pub, situated just off today's busy A275 between Offham and Lewes, it comprised waggons controlled by a cable operated on a funicular principle on a slope between a chalk pit and a canal spur. Barges on the Ouse Canal below waited to take the chalk or lime to its destination. The adviser and planner for the idea was William Jessop.

Since the gradient of the incline was 1 in 2, Jessop foresaw there would be difficulties in controlling the downward speed so he suggested a 'fly or fanner' to be attached to the waggons. This would look like a large aeroplane propeller which would have a 'parachute brake' effect and allow descent at a regulated speed. Jessop little realised this was to be the forerunner to the reverse thrust principle used by some aircraft when landing today. A brick tunnel still exists which passes under the A275, the upper entrance being close to the pub itself.

Interest moved northwards following George Stephenson's enthusiasm over steam engines. With the opening of the Stockton to Darlington Railway in 1825, the first steam train had arrived. In the same year an Act was granted for the Canterbury & Whitstable Railway to be built. In 1826 a line between Manchester and Liverpool was approved and three years later the famous Rainhill trials took place to establish which type of steam engine gave the best means of traction.

Travelling was pretty uncomfortable in those early days. Railway carriages began as stage-coach bodies attached to waggon bases. They were small, cramped and unlit and had no heating or travel facilities. When lighting came it was by oil lamps, subsequently to be replaced by gas lamps. Steam heating and comfortable seating came late in the century although the 1880s saw the introduction of dining cars equipped with kitchens for long distance travel. It is a sad reflection of our times that the luxuries of Pullman car travel are today almost defunct!

The first line to be opened for conventional trains in Sussex was between Brighton and Shoreham on 12th May 1840. A service between London and Brighton followed on 21st September 1841. The line to the coast had taken three years to build. During its construction some 3,500 men and 570 horses had been used.

Further railway lines throughout Sussex were to follow. By 1846 trains reached Chichester to the west and St Leonards to the east. Portsmouth via Havant was reached a year later and a branch line from Lewes to Newhaven Wharf was completed in the same year.

As the railways continued so the canals lost trade through direct competition, particularly since numerous lines were built parallel to them. In addition, by the 1840s many miles of road throughout the county had been turnpiked and road surfaces gradually improved. The waterways had no hope and all were to be abandoned commercially by the end of the 19th century. Despite the improved roads, it became quicker and easier to move freight by rail. Freight depots were built and goods traffic became a feature at almost every station. Few stations, however small, were without sidings as business continued to increase. Truly the railways had come to Sussex!

The majority of these have served a useful life, some lasting over a century and a half and, of course, many live actively on. This book intends to cover those lines which did not survive in their original form.

Leslie Oppitz

1
A Line To The East

Three Bridges to East Grinstead

A Q class 0-6-0 no 30543 approaches East Grinstead High Level from Oxted on 22nd May 1948. A line to Three Bridges leaves to the left. (John H. Meredith)

By the middle of the 19th century East Grinstead was a thriving market town. It was this, among other factors, that influenced John Urpeth Rastrick, already renowned for his work on the London to Brighton line, to submit a scheme for a branch line from Three Bridges to East Grinstead.

Earliest ideas of such a line came in 1845 when proposals were made to link the ports of Portsmouth, Chatham and Sheerness by rail. The Portsmouth section was to be covered by the London & South Western Railway (LSWR) joining a proposed

London, Brighton & South Coast Railway (LBSCR) line from Horsham to Three Bridges. The Brighton company would continue to East Grinstead and the South Eastern Railway (SER) wanted involvement in the remaining routes.

Many discussions and disagreements followed and it was not until 1846 that Parliament agreed that the LBSCR could go ahead with the East Grinstead branch line. No work proceeded and six years later in 1852 fresh proposals were submitted by an independent East Grinstead Railway Company. In the same year the new company approached the LBSCR seeking a working arrangement whereby the LBSCR used the independent company's line for an annual rental of £2,000 for 999 years. The East Grinstead Company then sought authorisation based on a capital of £50,000 with the LBSCR reserving the right to purchase the local company for such a sum. Traffic was expected to be lively and construction costs were reckoned around £47,000.

A tender of £43,700 was accepted from George Wythes of Reigate for construction of the line. Further delays occurred when Mr Wilson, a landowner east of Rowfant, objected to a railway across his property but this was resolved in 1855. The line opened for traffic on the 9th of July of the same year, nine years after it had been approved. The company was taken over by the LBSCR in 1861.

Trains left Three Bridges from platform six, a bay at the south end of the station. The bay and its track have long since gone, making way for a signalling computer centre which controls most of the London to Brighton track. With a Three Bridges to Horsham line already in existence, Three Bridges became an important junction. This is an area that grew with the railways although there are records of its existence as far back as 1613 when it was known as 'Le three bridges', believed to be referring to the number of bridges between Worth and Crawley.

As railway traffic increased, engine sheds were built and employment became widely available. Houses were built for the railwaymen at the foot of Station Hill and later in North Road and Three Bridges Road. New Street was built in the 1860s and

Three Bridges station, c1910. East Grinstead trains left the main Brighton line beyond to the left and Horsham trains to the right. (Lens of Sutton)

Three Bridges in LBSCR days. It is believed the station acquired its name from as far back as 1613 when the area was known as 'Le three bridges', referring to the number of bridges between Worth and Crawley. (Lens of Sutton)

as its name implies was the first new road to be built. The railway line from London to Brighton was widened at Three Bridges to four tracks in 1907 to cope with increased traffic. The widening was carried out between Earlswood and the north portal of Balcombe tunnel. There were plans to take it through to Brighton but circumstances and costs never allowed this. The main drawbacks were the need to build second tunnels at Balcombe and Clayton, plus shorter ones at Haywards Heath and Patcham alongside the present ones and also to widen or double the Ouse Valley Viaduct.

When the extra tracks went through Three Bridges, the old tunnel arch over the road was replaced by the present girder bridge. The goods shed and Longley's yard were cleared to make way for a new station building built in 1911. The engine sheds were relocated further south beyond the fork made by the line to Horsham.

The Three Bridges to East Grinstead branch line was single track and seven miles long. Originally there was only one halt, at Rowfant. Grange Road station followed in 1860 to serve nearby Crawley Down. When trains began there were six each way on weekdays and two each way on Sundays. Initially traffic exceeded expectations and by the next year there were nine trains each way daily and three on Sundays. By 1865, ten years after its opening, the LBSCR, in accordance with its contract with the East Grinstead Company, took up its option to take over the entire line.

Leaving Three Bridges station, the line curved sharply eastwards towards Compasses level crossing, so called after an adjacent inn. Over the years several early goods trains found themselves ploughing their way through closed wooden gates, when perhaps the keeper in the adjacent cottage failed to make the early hour! The first stop was at Rowfant which had two platforms so that trains could pass. The main building was Tudoresque and stood adjacent to a level crossing where the road crossed the line at an oblique angle. The station was built to serve nearby Rowfant House and the main building included a small porch at the level crossing end. This was provided as a

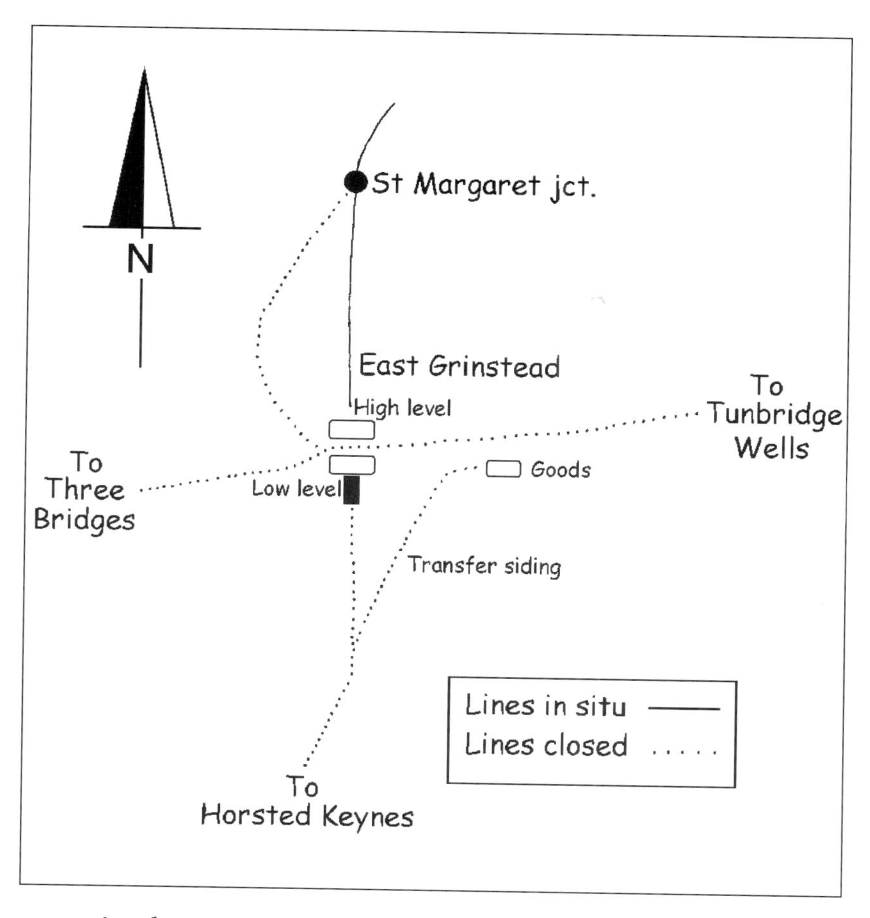

cover for the owner of Rowfant House should he have to await his carriage for the journey home.

Grange Road has today been completely obliterated by shops and houses. This was another station named after a nearby house, the Grange, which was ¾ mile to the south of the line. Unlike Rowfant, there was no passing loop and the station comprised a platform, a level crossing and a signal box. Two miles to the east where Imberhorne Lane crossed the line, there

Rowfant station in LBSCR days. The porch at the end of the building used to shelter the owner of Rowfant House whilst he awaited his carriage. (Lens of Sutton)

Grange Road station, c1910. The station comprised a platform, level crossing and signal box and it was named after nearby Grange House. (Lens of Sutton)

was a private siding built to serve the then Imberhorne Estate. This closed in 1948.

The first East Grinstead station, opened in 1855, was a terminus in Station Approach Road, now Railway Approach. The original station building is still in use as a private dwelling. When a line to Tunbridge Wells opened in 1866 the station moved north to under the London Road where today passes the aptly named 'Beeching Way'.

By 1882 East Grinstead was built at its present location as a two-level station. The branch from the Three Bridges line straddled a line from Lewes which extended northwards to Oxted two years later in 1884. The High Level station is now demolished and forms a car park to the west of the present station. It was from this area that a loop was opened in 1884 so that trains from Tunbridge Wells could branch northwards to join the line to Oxted, giving a through service to London via East Grinstead. In 1879 a proposal had been authorised to

The now-demolished East Grinstead High Level station looking towards Forest Row and photographed not long before its closure in the 1960s. (Lens of Sutton)

Three trains await departure at East Grinstead High Level on 15th March 1958. Locomotives are nos 30534, 31329 and 31350. (John H. Meredith)

provide a further loop from the Oxted line to allow through running to Three Bridges but this was never done.

In January 1967 the last train left Three Bridges for East Grinstead and Tunbridge Wells. Only a section of track from Three Bridges to Rowfant remained for a short time serving a depot at Rowfant.

A walk along the old track, Worth Way, is recommended. An OS map is needed to circumnavigate the new developments particularly at Grange Road. Otherwise the walk is straight-forward and well signposted all the way. Areas are becoming overgrown and can be very muddy but it is worth the effort. Best remains on the route are at Rowfant where the station building plus porch still exist although now part of Colas, a company of tarmac distributors.

The line from East Grinstead northwards, at one time considered 'doomed', showed new lease of life when electric services were introduced on 30th September 1987 linking at South Croydon with

Rowfant station building today has become part of the Colas company, tarmac distributors. The platform, signal box and track have all gone. (Author)

A Connex South Central train awaits departure from East Grinstead. The brick wall on the far side of the platform at one time served as one of the buttresses to support the High Level station. (Author)

the main London-Brighton line. In the not too distant future trains will arrive again from Kingscote giving the present-day Bluebell its planned link with the town. A station which once served four different directions is truly coming back to life.

2
The Lewes And Uckfield Railway Co

Lewes to Uckfield
The Lavender Line

Isfield station on the Uckfield to Lewes line in LBSCR days. There has been talk that the line from Uckfield to Lewes might reopen to regular traffic but much would need to be done. (Lens of Sutton)

Lewes to Uckfield

An announcer at East Croydon calls, 'The Semi-Fast Electric Train now standing at this platform will call at Oxted, Crowborough, Uckfield, Lewes and Brighton'. Fanciful perhaps? We already hear that electrification of the Oxted to Uckfield line is a possibility and if local pressure groups backing the Wealden Line Campaign have their way then the Uckfield to

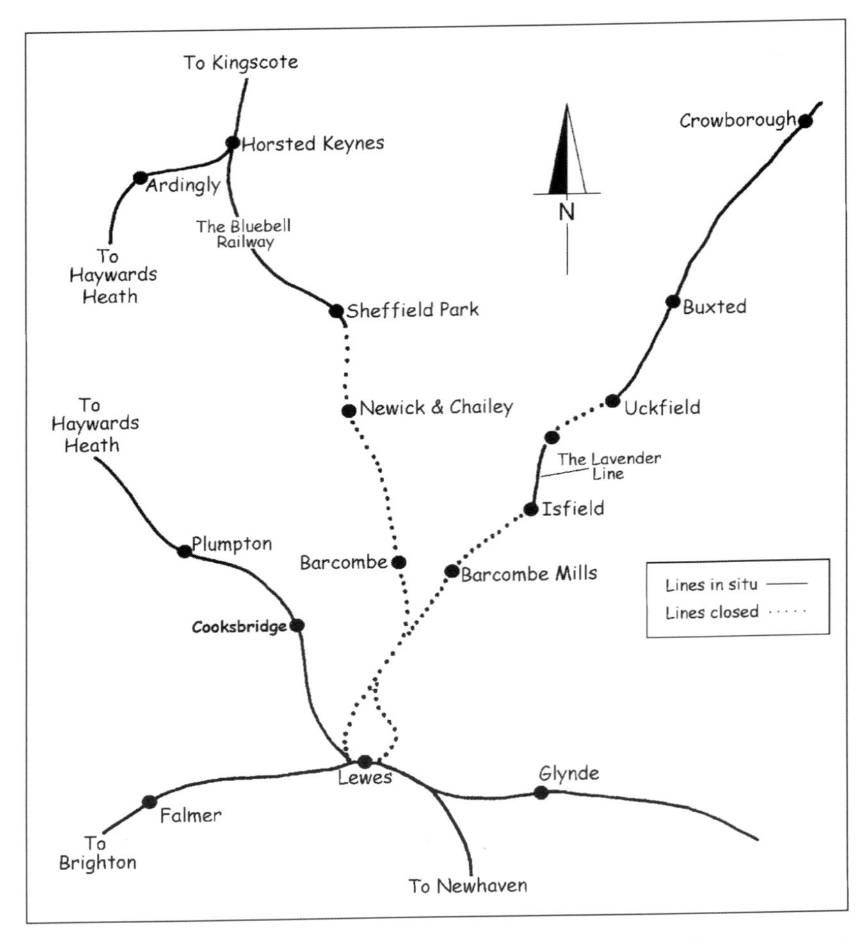

Lewes section, closed in 1969, will be restored. The trackbed between Uckfield and Lewes remains relatively clear and it is well ballasted. Modern tracklaying equipment would ensure that relaying the line would not prove a great obstacle. The problem of crossing the Uckfield bypass would need to be overcome and provision would need to be made to ensure that Isfield's Lavender Line is preserved in some way.

Ideas for a line from Uckfield to Lewes were first put forward in 1844. With Uckfield being an agricultural centre of some importance and Lewes being the county town of East Sussex, it was considered that such a link was necessary. Nothing tangible happened at that time and it was not until the mid 1850s that further moves took place. A local company called the Lewes and Uckfield Railway Co was formed and permission was granted for it to proceed by means of an Act dated 27th July 1856.

Lewes's first railway station was built in 1846 at Friar's Walk when the Brighton, Lewes & Hastings Railway was constructed. Two smaller stations also existed being Ham or Southover (fairly near the present station) and Pinwell just south of Friar's Walk on the line to Hastings. All this soon became part of the London, Brighton & South Coast Railway (LBSCR) which, by the next year, had taken over the line and opened another between Lewes and Keymer Junction (just south of Wivelsfield) on the main London to Brighton route. The Lewes & Uckfield Railway Act was passed in 1856 and Lewes station was resited the following year in anticipation of increased traffic. It was built close to the present one and Friar's Walk station was relegated to goods traffic only.

The Lewes to Uckfield line opened on 18th October 1858. Initially a service of five trains each way was provided daily with only three on Sundays. In 1859 the branch was taken over by the LBSCR. For the first ten years Uckfield-bound trains left the Lewes to Keymer Junction line at Uckfield Junction just north of Lewes. This meant that trains travelling from Uckfield on through to Brighton had to reverse at Lewes. To overcome this a new track was built in 1868 giving access to Lewes from the east.

Travelling towards Uckfield the first station northwards was Barcombe Mills. Originally known as Barcombe, this was sited nearly a mile south-east of an area which comprised more a cluster of hamlets than anything else. Surprisingly Barcombe was to be served by two stations when the East Grinstead line was completed.

Barcombe could have become involved in a third railway

route. At a time when the LBSCR was expanding eastwards, the London, Chatham and Dover Railway (LCDR) had ideas on the Brighton territory. Such ideas were strengthened when the LCDR joined forces with the South Eastern Railway (SER) to plan a route southwards from Beckenham to Lewes and Brighton. It was proposed such a line should pass through Horsted Keynes and Sheffield Park (later to become part of the Bluebell Line) and then through Barcombe to enter the north-west of Lewes. Beyond Lewes it would have negotiated two tunnels to Rottingdean, then westwards to Brighton to a rival terminus at the Steine. History tells us of course that this did not happen.

Before leaving Barcombe, the waterways are worth investigating. These are located east of the former station along the old road and close to where one of the oldest tollgates in the country existed. A more up-to-date list of charges can still be seen on a board fixed to the building and it is said tolls were first levied there in 1066. Barcombe Mills has always been a favourite for anglers and on a bank holiday before the last war as many as 1,000 railway tickets were sold in one day.

After Barcombe Mills came Isfield. During the First World War, milk churns came by rail to Isfield. This was a time when passers-by were warned of a train approaching by the ringing of a handbell from the signal box. The trains also brought German POWs to Isfield for forestry work in the Plashett Wood area. At the end of the day the POWs were marched back to the station for a return to camp.

When Uckfield opened over 140 years ago it had two platforms, each with buildings, and it halted just short of the main road. It was destined to become an important rail centre with passenger and goods traffic. Freight had previously reached Uckfield from a cut off the Ouse Canal up the River Uck where it terminated at Shortbridge. The original terminal basin, now overgrown, can be traced only half a mile south of the Peacock Inn along a public footpath by a road junction.

It was not long before the Lewes to Uckfield line was used for through services from Brighton to Tunbridge Wells. This was a

Lewes station has recently been renovated to a high standard. Tracks to the left serve trains to Brighton while trains to Plumpton, Wivelsfield and Haywards Heath leave to the right. (Author)

Barcombe Mills station on the former Lewes to Uckfield line closed completely in 1969. Since that time the station buildings have included a florist and the 'Wheel Tappers Restaurant'. (Author)

Staff and passengers pose on the up platform at Isfield station in the early 1900s. The line opened in October 1858 and lasted 111 years to regular passenger traffic. (Lens of Sutton)

further part of the Brighton company's strategy to consolidate the area against competition from the east. To allow such through services a loop was opened between Eridge and Groombridge, the latter station already in existence on the East Grinstead to Tunbridge Wells route. When a further line opened from Polegate to Eridge in 1880 the LBSCR had achieved its objective.

Frequent trains to Tunbridge Wells, East Grinstead and Lewes and beyond were now possible. These survived until well into this century. Perhaps Uckfield station's heyday was in the late 1930s when a daily through service existed between Brighton, Maidstone and Chatham to the east and Brighton, Redhill and Reading to the west.

By the 1960s the Beeching era had begun and in 1964 the timetables were recast making travel difficult, by now a common ploy to reduce the number of passengers. The Railway Board wanted closure between Groombridge and Lewes. This met with vigorous opposition from local authorities and private individuals. Eventually the Minister gave way and agreed closure between Uckfield and Lewes only. The date was fixed for 6th January 1969.

Bickering followed and the licensing of replacement buses was deferred. The Railway Board claimed that a viaduct across the River Ouse was safe only on one line and a shuttle service was introduced. This did not fit in with trains north of Uckfield and traffic dropped still further. Eventually railway engineers insisted the viaduct should be completely closed.

The railways then hired buses for a time and Barcombe Mills and Isfield stayed open to issue tickets. The buses could not negotiate the narrow winding road to Barcombe Mills, so the railways had to provide a taxi to take passengers from the railway station to the bus stop. But this was only after intending passengers had walked over a mile to the station to buy their tickets!

The last train ran on 23rd February 1969 and buses stopped on 6th May 1969. Today Uckfield station building is no longer there. It survived until the end of 2000 by which time the trackbed had become totally overgrown with buddleia taking over. Sadly the floods of autumn 2000 together with vandals and arsonists proved too much and demolition became necessary. Today's station is sited on the opposite side of the road thus relieving motorists frustrated over the years who had to wait each time a train crossed. The signal box is still there. It serves as an office to Minack Mechanical Maintenance Ltd.

Visiting Lewes station today one is immediately struck by the general tidiness and colourful paintwork. The original Friar's Walk station was completely demolished in the 1960s and a magistrates court built on the site. The area which once carried the Uckfield line out of the town has been redeveloped with new shops and a car park.

Barcombe Mills station is still there and the remains of a level crossing gate can be seen forgotten in the undergrowth on the northern side. Since closure, the station's buildings became a florists on the down side and the 'Wheel Tappers Restaurant' on the other. A notice reading 'Beware of Trains' has sadly lost its meaning.

Uckfield station prior to its resiting to the east of the main road. (R.K. Blencowe)

Uckfield station has been moved to the east side of the main road so that the level crossing can be removed and traffic can flow freely. (Author)

Uckfield's earlier signal box still survives close to the road. It is used as office accommodation by Minack Mechanical Maintenance Ltd. (Author)

After closure of the line the platforms at Isfield were neglected and the track removed. The platforms, buildings and signal box survived but despite this local folk could have thought that was the end as far as trains were concerned. Fourteen years later they were to be proved wrong.

The Lavender Line

In 1983 the Milham family purchased Isfield station and efforts to restore it to its former state met with success. Called the Lavender Line, track was relaid and rolling stock purchased. It got its name because coal merchants A.E. Lavender & Sons of Ringmer used to operate from the station yard. The first locomotive came from a paper mill up north. It was a 1903 Barclay 0-4-0 saddle tank locomotive that had been restored

D3 class 0-4-4T at Isfield station, c 1905. The station closed in 1969, the platforms became neglected and the track was removed. Efforts to restore the station began in 1983 and it is today well known as the Lavender Line. (Lens of Sutton)

Isfield station July 1983 in a dilapidated state shortly before the station was reopened by David Milham and his family. The trackbed had become completely overgrown. (Author)

over a period of eight years by the Bury Transport Museum.

The arrival of another locomotive in August 1984 caused much local excitement. It was a 2-10-0 WD class used extensively in the last war. Built in 1943, it went into 'active service' after D-Day pulling Red Cross trains in Normandy. After the war it went to Greece and became a snowplough in the north of the country. Almost exactly one year after arrival at Isfield, on 6th August 1985, the fully refurbished locomotive was the object of a visit by Dame Vera Lynn when she gave it her name. In May 1986 the locomotive was purchased by Clifford Brown, a wealthy American ironworks owner, who bought it as a 40th wedding anniversary present for his wife! After a short stay at the Mid-Hants Railway, the *Dame Vera Lynn* left for the North Yorkshire Moors Railway where it will probably remain.

David Milham pulled out in 1992 at which point a group of enthusiasts formed a Society and took over. In no more than 15 months, membership reached around 300 although finance

The ex-WD 2-10-0 locomotive no 3672 'Dame Vera Lynn' photographed at the North Yorkshire Moors Railway at Grosmont on 8th August 1990. The locomotive began its UK existence when it was restored at Isfield, arriving in 1984. (John H. Meredith)

remained a problem. The station house was sold as well as two coaches used on an earlier 'wine and dine' operation. The Society was able to retain two small steam locomotives, *Austerity* 0-6-0ST no 68012 and Barclay 0-4-0ST *Annie*. Much still needed to be done.

When visited by the author in September 2000 there was ample activity at Isfield despite poor weather. The principle motive power for the day was a class 73 Bo-Bo E6003 *Sir Herbert Walker*. During the year 2000 delivery was taken on an ex-Connex 09 shunter, vacuum and air braked. Restoration of the former LBSCR signal box is an ongoing project, a working railway museum can be visited as well as a gift shop on platform 2. The former booking hall welcomes visitors as the 'Cinders Buffet'.

Following acquisition of the Connex South Central franchise by a new company, GOVIA (a joint venture between the Go-

Trains stand in Isfield station, today the headquarters of the Lavender Railway Preservation Society. It acquired its name from the coal merchants, A.E.Lavender & Sons of Ringmer, which operated from the station yard. (Author)

Looking northwards from Isfield where much damage was done to the Lavender Line during the floods of October 2000. The sleepers weigh ¼ ton each! (Rod Peters)

Ahead Bus Group and the French company Via Carianne), the possibility that the Lewes to Uckfield line might be reinstated has receded into the distant future. Maybe in future years it will be Lavender Line trains that will first reach Uckfield from the south.

An extract from a book called *The England I Love Best* by James Turle, written in 1934, reads as follows: 'If I were a rich man, I think I would buy Isfield station from the Southern Railway, and have it for my own, my very own. There are quieter stations, there are some isolated stations, stations set amid more romantic scenery, but there is no station quite like Isfield . . .'

3
Battles Along The Adur Valley

Christ's Hospital to Shoreham

D3 class 0-4-4T no 32364 hauls a down passenger train from Christ's Hospital in 1950. In the far distance, lines leave for Guildford. (Lens of Sutton)

A railway from Shoreham to Steyning was first considered in 1846. Perhaps because Steyning's population at that time was less than 1,500 the idea gained little headway. In 1856 the idea was revived since, with Lancing College under construction, a good revenue was contemplated. Others saw such a line extending to Henfield and on to West Grinstead which was the terminus of the Adur Navigation and the Baybridge Canal. The local and wealthy Burrell family, which had already made possible toll roads and the Baybridge Canal, assisted once again with offers of finance but insufficient capital to go ahead was raised.

The battle for the Adur Valley began in earnest on 15th December 1857, when a group of landowners formed the Shoreham, Horsham & Dorking Railway (SHDR). A meeting was held at the Burrell Arms at Shoreham to consider a 17 mile branch line from Horsham to the coast.

The LBSCR saw this as a threat to its existing coastal route and held a meeting on the same day at the George Inn, Henfield. The Chairman, Mr Leo Schuster, claimed that the SHDR was missing out Henfield by siting the railway on the other side of the river and a station proposed at Steyning would be a mile from the village. The LBSCR also threw doubts on the rival company's intention to link up the line with Leatherhead and Dorking. In the *West Sussex Gazette* of 14th January 1858, the SHDR claimed that much of the LBSCR's information was false and, indeed, said some of the correspondence had been faked.

Both Bills reached the House of Commons by April 1858. The LBSCR promised stations at Bramber (with the attraction of the castle), Steyning, Henfield (only ¼ mile from the church), Partridge Green, Shipley and Itchingfield. It was considered that the LBSCR had put a good case in the interests of Sussex people and the SHDR proposal was rejected. The LBSCR line was authorised on 12th July 1858 at an estimated cost of £155,000. One of the clauses in the contract stipulated that a light should be exhibited on the Adur Bridge at Coombes for guidance to shipping. Failure to comply carried a penalty of £10 per night. The line opened to its full length on 16th September 1861. The company was enthusiastic with four stopping trains and one express each way daily. The single track was doubled within 18 years.

Links between Steyning and Pulborough were frequently discussed and in 1864 the newly formed West Sussex Junction Railway was authorised to construct a line from Hardham to Steyning.

An even bolder branch line was approved by Parliament in the same year to link West Grinstead, Cuckfield and Haywards Heath at an estimated cost of £110,000. Perhaps Cuckfield, which had once rejected the London to Brighton line within its

Christ's Hospital station in steam days. On the right is the loop line that served the nearby Bluecoat school. (Lens of Sutton)

boundaries, had the same feelings over this new proposal. Both the ideas were rejected.

The line from Christ's Hospital to Shoreham left the main line between Horsham and Pulborough just south of Christ's Hospital station at Itchingfield junction almost on the perimeter of the school playing fields. The area was not without its place in railway history. There was a fatal accident at Itchingfield junction in 1866 when at least one man died following a collision between two passenger trains. Another bad accident occurred there on 5th March 1964. It was early morning when a Brighton to Three Bridges freight, diverted via Henfield due to engineering works, ran into the side of the Three Bridges to Chichester freight. The northbound diesel ploughed through the trucks in its path, flinging them some 50 ft into the air. It came to rest in the field opposite and its crew were killed.

During the Second World War the lines of West Sussex were under frequent attack. In 1942 a Horsham to Steyning freight train was machine-gunned by a German aircraft and the driver died from his wounds.

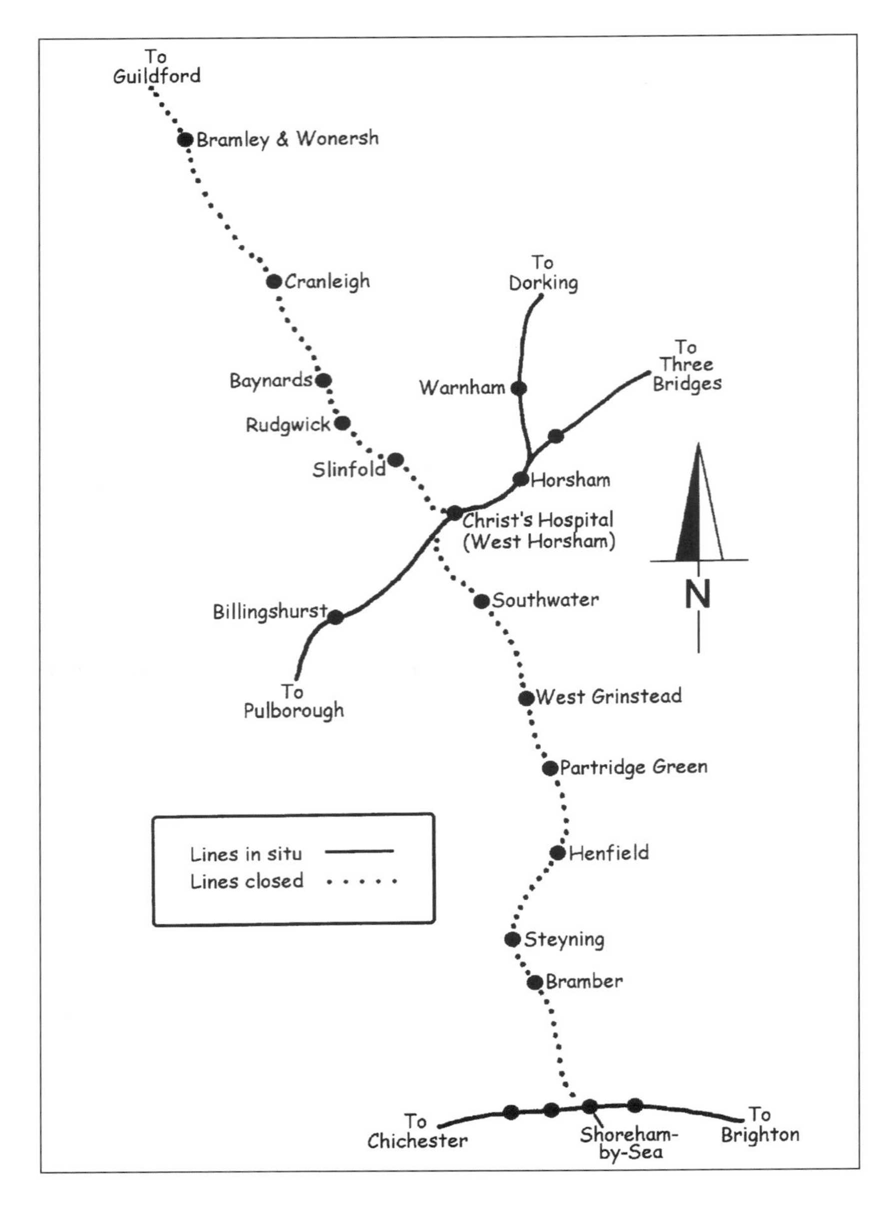
To
Guildford
Bramley & Wonersh
Cranleigh
To
Dorking
Baynards
Warnham
To
Three
Bridges
Rudgwick
Slinfold
Horsham
Christ's Hospital
(West Horsham)
N
Billingshurst
Southwater
To
Pulborough
West Grinstead
Partridge Green
Lines in situ
Lines closed
Henfield
Steyning
Bramber
To
Chichester
Shoreham-
by-Sea
To
Brighton

K class 2-6-0 locomotive no 32337 photographed approaching Southwater station. This was a Stephenson Locomotive Society special, run on 23rd June 1956. (John H. Meredith)

South of Christ's Hospital the first stop was Southwater. The station stood central to the village, but today only a bare platform has survived. A nameboard there reminds passers-by that a station once covered the site. Today not only is the platform silent; the main A24 traffic has been diverted away from the village by the A24 bypass.

Nearly three miles further on lies West Grinstead. This was a little-used station built in a sparse locality over a mile from the village. The old LBSCR station building still exists being close to what was the Tabby Cat inn (now a Little Chef restaurant) on the A272. The trackbed is currently part of the South Downs Way and Sussex County Council have installed a signal by the platform and a coach on a short stretch of track to recall the past.

A visit to the parish church at West Grinstead is recommended. This is a delightfully isolated spot close to the River Adur. It was this stretch of water that in 1825 formed part of the Baybridge Canal before the railways arrived. This was

The up side station building at Southwater on 10th July 1965. The line closed in March 1966. (John H. Meredith)

A Brighton to Horsham train arrives at Southwater on 10th July 1965. After closure the station area was used for a time by a local horticultural society. (John H. Meredith)

constructed to make the river navigable for a further three miles upstream to Bay Bridge near the remains of Knepp Castle on the present A24. Here a terminal basin was constructed where barges would complete their journey and await their return. In the churchyard at West Grinstead is a tombstone of one of the wealthy Burrell family who helped to finance this canal when it was constructed. The waterway lasted a mere 35 years and was abandoned when the railways came.

Partridge Green station is lost under a new housing estate but a bridge on the B2135 over what was a railway track remains. Partridge Green, like West Grinstead, was a small village and traffic was slight. The station opened on 1st July 1861 and was for a short time the northern end of the line from Shoreham. The section northwards opened in September of the same year.

Long before the railways reached Henfield, the village had stood on a prominent route for coaches and horses between London and Brighton. In addition, the road carried traffic westwards towards Guildford and Windsor and was used a great deal by George, Prince Regent and later King. Henfield

Partridge Green station in earlier times. The station area today is lost under a housing estate but an overbridge on the B2135 remains. (Lens of Sutton)

LBSCR E4 class 0-6-2T no 50 waits at Henfield with a down passenger train, c1910. (Lens of Sutton)

High Street must have been a busy place with coaches constantly passing through or stopping at the posting houses, the George, the Plough and the White Hart.

It is said that the White Hart dates back as early as 1543 – back to the time of Henry VIII's reign. It stood then on a toll route south from Guildford. After a change of horses and tea for the travellers, the journey would resume via Poynings to finish at the Metropole in Brighton.

Steyning throughout the centuries has always been an important town. In Norman times, before the River Adur silted up, it was a prominent Channel coast port. It was known as St Cuthman's, probably named after the shepherd saint who built his church there in the 8th century. By the 14th century the estuary had become a wide expanse of salt marsh which stretched between the villages of Bramber and Beeding. This was crossed by a very long causeway and a bridge.

At the beginning of the 16th century the river banks were built up. During the last century it was possible to visualise how the sea once reached Steyning during the extensive flooding of the

Steyning station not long before closure. The station has been demolished but the goods warehouse on the right has survived. (Lens of Sutton)

At the former Steyning station these five residences were previously a goods depository. The area is today known as Market Square. (Author)

An LBSCR tank locomotive hauling a passenger set approaches Bramber station. After closure of the line the station area gave way to a large roundabout that diverts traffic from the village. (Lens of Sutton)

Henfield station closed in 1966 to be later replaced by a housing estate which includes a road called 'Beechings'. (Author)

river in 1924–25. To the north of the railway station the flood water formed a wide creek which indicated the place where the little ships would load and unload somewhat to the east of the church. Further evidence to this effect is said to be the accumulation of shingle which, at one time, existed as far up the river valley as east of the railway station. At Bramber it is said that traces of a landing quay came to light during the 19th century, almost opposite the steps leading to the church and castle.

Trains along the Adur Valley lasted 105 years. The last train to reach Steyning station carried a wreath on the buffers reading 'In loving memory of the faithful'. The A283 now covers the track that once linked Bramber with Steyning. Travelling past Steyning, the old goods warehouse can be seen but the station has been demolished. The goods warehouse has become five private residences located in Market Square.

Bramber station has long since gone to make way for the large roundabout that diverts traffic from the village. From Bramber the track followed the river down the valley, past sidings to Beeding cement works, to join the coast route at Shoreham.

For a time diesel units were used to prolong its life and the route became known as the 'linger and die' line. But even this move did not save the situation and despite stormy protest meetings the inevitable came about and the Adur Valley line closed on 17th March 1966 leaving only a single track line from Shoreham to Beeding.

When the railways left Henfield, perhaps the greatest injustice to railway enthusiasts was to call the new road on the site of the station 'Beechings'.

4
Lines To The West

Pulborough to Midhurst

An ex-LBSCR D1 class 0-4-2T and an ex-SWR M7 class 0-4-4T no 27 at Midhurst station. (Lens of Sutton)

With the main London to Brighton line opened in 1841 and the west coastway route from Brighton to Portsmouth completed six years later, a large part of West Sussex was now ripe for development. Horsham was reached from Three Bridges in 1848 and with this in mind a local company, called the Mid Sussex Railway, had ideas to build a line from Horsham via Billingshurst and Pulborough to Petworth.

At the Horsham end of the line the intention was to build an end-on junction with the LBSCR line. It had been proposed to reach as far as Midhurst but funds had not permitted. The Mid Sussex Railway received Royal Assent to proceed on 10th August 1857. Another company, the Mid Sussex and Midhurst, received approval in an Act dated 13th August 1859 to cover the Petworth to Midhurst section.

Both companies were under the LBSCR's auspices and it was originally the intention to extend westwards to Petersfield. The LBSCR did not support this, pointing out it was contrary to an agreement with the London & South Western Railway (LSWR). The LBSCR's support of other companies had aroused strong LSWR suspicion of incursions into what it considered its territory. Matters were finally resolved following meetings held between the rival companies in 1860 and 1862.

Initially it had been planned that the line should be built directly from Billingshurst to Petworth rather than via Pulborough. The proposal was that instead of curving south out of Billingshurst village, the line would continue straight from opposite Daux Farm (now the Daux Road area) and pass by way of Wisborough Green and Kirdford to a terminus north of Petworth which was ¾ mile from the town centre and not 1½ miles to the south as eventually occurred. This route, however, would have required a 25 ft span bridge and an 18 ft clearance over the canal at Orfold Lock near Wisborough Green.

There was much argument for and against both a direct Billingshurst to Petworth route and a route via Pulborough. This latter line would follow the south bank of the lower Rother Valley. Landowners and the Arun Navigation became involved and at one stage the Duke of Norfolk gave evidence.

The line from Horsham to Petworth opened on 15th October 1859. Horsham station was not constructed end-on as originally planned but was built so through trains were possible. The line was initially built as a single track and the intermediate stations were thought to have been of two platforms with crossing loops.

At Billingshurst the principal station buildings and a goods yard were all built on the up side. When services began a level crossing existed immediately west of the station. Between Horsham and Billingshurst alone there were some 25 level crossings although many were later closed. Others in the area had unexpected names such as Daux crossing, east of the village (named after the farm), Rats Bottom crossing a mile west of Adversane and Frogshole footpath near the Cray Lane road crossing.

A mile to the east of Billingshurst station the line passed over a two-span bridge. One of these crossed a stream and the other was provided for accommodation purposes. This latter was unusual in that the railway was not to be responsible for the maintenance. This was agreed at a meeting held on 28th March 1859 between the Mid Sussex Railway Company and Thomas Wisden Esq. The two-span bridge became known as Pot Porridge Bridge (or sometimes Porridge Pot Bridge).

The journey from Horsham to Billingshurst took 20 minutes. According to local newspaper reports in the early days, railway employees selected for the station were somewhat displeased when they found '. . . it was rustically situated in a ploughed field'. One surprised porter was said to have asked, 'Where's the village?' Eventually Billingshurst was connected by a proper road to its station and a hotel was provided.

The village itself has never been considered isolated, having been situated on the long stretch of Roman road known as Stane Street. It is sometimes called 'Old Nick's road' for, an elderly local once said, 'How else would it have been so straight?' The myth had evolved locally that the Devil himself had made the road straight so that he might despatch the sinful along it to perdition more swiftly. May one here presume that perdition was the Capital?

At Pulborough the single track line to Petworth started from a loop on the west side of the station.

Pulborough station originally comprised three facing platforms, numerous sidings, a turntable, a goods shed and a signal box. Nearby was a busy cattle market and cattle pens stood adjacent to the siding on the west side. On the platforms were water towers to supply the engines.

Immediately south of Pulborough there was trouble building a bridge to cross the River Arun. The piers of the bridge continually sank and eventually all the supports had to be

Pulborough looking northwards. The station was once a junction providing trains to Petworth and Midhurst as well as the South Coast. The branch to Midhurst closed in the mid-1950s. (Author)

Hardham junction signal box and level crossing photographed on 11th March 1965 where a line to Midhurst left the Pulborough main line to the coast. (John H. Meredith)

abolished and work had to begin again. The Petworth line bore west to Fittleworth just south of Hardham Mill where Hardham junction was built in 1859 for a line to Arundel.

Fittleworth station opened 30 years later in 1889. It had a single platform with a plain wooden canopy and a siding. There was no passing loop. It lay just over half a mile south of the village and just off the present B2138, south of two river bridges. Nearby are two LBSCR stucco railway cottages. Fittleworth station building became dilapidated after closure of the line but today it is tastefully restored and privately owned.

Petworth station was reached a further 2½ miles westward, sited by an overbridge on the busy A285 and close to Coultershaw Mill. For seven years this was a terminus but unfortunately for prospective travellers it was sited 1½ miles south of the town. A new inn was built by the station but this could only serve to postpone the walk home! A local person of

Fittleworth station between Pulborough and Petworth was a latecomer to the line, opening in 1889. It had a single platform and there was no passing loop. (R.K. Blencowe)

much enterprise ran an omnibus to meet all trains but at 6d a ride this would seem expensive for the time.

Initially five trains a day reached Petworth and a journey from Three Bridges took one and a quarter hours. Only a week after the line was opened its success was marked by a special excursion train to Crystal Palace for a return fare of 3s 6d including admission to the Exhibition.

The six mile Petworth to Midhurst stretch was opened on 15th October 1866. Two years earlier the first trains had reached Midhurst from Petersfield on lines controlled by the LSWR so pressure had grown on the LBSCR to complete the link. In all it had taken the LBSCR, in conjunction with the Midhurst and Mid Sussex Junction Railway, seven years between authorisation and completion.

There had been construction problems. The Midhurst tunnel gave difficulties and a man had been hurt by a fall of earth. The

Petworth station looking towards Pulborough, 24th July 1955. Goods traffic survived between Petworth and Pulborough until May 1966. (John H. Meredith)

local press were highly critical over the delays. 'Wonders will never cease', said the *West Sussex Gazette* on 15th October 1866, 'the Petworth and Midhurst Railway, alias 'Death's line', was opened on Monday. This project has been so long in hand we began to despair. . .'

The agreement for the line to Midhurst stipulated that a station should be opened at Selham but this did not happen until 1872. Today the station is private property and cannot be approached. It was a wooden building with only one platform and had no passing loop. Standing on a high embankment west of a road it was near a pub called The Three Moles.

With Midhurst approached from east and west there was now a continuous rail link from Horsham (with its London connections) and Petersfield, mostly on LBSCR rails. Even this had its problems as Midhurst now had two railway stations. A rail connection was brought into use on 17th December 1866, but since a bridge between the two was too weak for locomotives, waggons were transferred by horse power and the

An LBSCR locomotive with mixed coaches arrives at Midhurst station. At one time Midhurst had two railway stations but these were amalgamated in 1925 by the Southern Railway. (Lens of Sutton)

public had to walk! The LBSCR station was later rebuilt further east when the line to Chichester was built in 1881. Two stations still existed and there were constant complaints. It was not until 1925 that the Southern Railway concentrated on the LBSCR station and closed the other.

On the line to Petersfield there were two intermediate stations. The first was at Elsted in an isolated situation and where once the platform stood there is now a new building housing offices and accommodation. The last station in Sussex was Rogate where the original plain platform building became a plastics factory.

The Midhurst stations are now lost in building development. The 1881 LBSCR station was located at the entrance to an estate off New Road leading to The Fairway, off the A286, the latter built over the trackbed up to Midhurst tunnel. The original LBSCR Midhurst station was just to the east of the Bepton Road underbridge (now demolished). The old LSWR station stood to the west of the underbridge and the area is now an industrial estate.

As usual the decline came in the 1950s. By this time trains were often running nearly empty particularly on Sundays. So the Sunday trains stopped in 1951 and all passenger services eventually ceased on 5th February 1955. West of Midhurst the line was completely closed but freight continued to Midhurst and Petworth until this was abandoned in October 1964. Between Petworth and Pulborough (Hardham junction) goods traffic lasted until May 1966.

At Petworth station today it is possible to recall earlier railway times. The station building is now a Grade II listed building, fully restored and offering a high standard of accommodation. The waiting room with its 20 ft vaulted ceiling and original ticket office windows has become a breakfast room and lounge. A spiral library leads to beamed upper bedrooms which are in addition to four individual suites in the two Pullman coaches in a short siding a few steps away.

These Pullmans, *Alicante* and *Mimosa,* were rescued after 35 years of neglect on a Cornish beach. They were built as First

Petworth station, originally built in 1894 and today a Grade II listed building, has been fully restored to become The Old Railway Station offering high quality accommodation. (Photograph courtesy of Mary-Lou Rapley)

Class parlour cars for the Pullman Car Company, *Alicante* in 1912 and *Mimosa* two years later. *Alicante* initially served with the South Eastern & Chatham Railway (SECR) and was used on regular runs between London and Margate or Ramsgate. The early history of *Mimosa* is not certain but it is known both were badly damaged by fire at a Battersea depot in 1935. After rebuilds they remained in service until 1961 to become camping coaches the following year. They finished up at Marazion in Cornwall together with four others where the sea air, vandals and looters soon took their toll.

But these forces had not reckoned with Mary-Lou Rapley who purchased *Alicante* and *Mimosa* and had them transported to Petworth's bay platform in September 1998. Their condition was appalling but Mary-Lou took up the challenge. Restoration

Two Pullman coaches at Petworth have been restored to become four individual suites with all comforts. The Pullmans were rescued after 35 years of neglect on a Cornish beach. (Photograph courtesy of Mary-Lou Rapley)

began in earnest with help and advice coming from many quarters including the Bluebell Railway. Roofs and bodies were repaired and the coaches were painted in Pullman umber and cream livery. Each vehicle was divided in the middle providing two en-suite bedrooms per car. The result is truly worth experiencing – a brochure adds, 'Romantic Champagne Breakfasts on Request'!

5
A Line Into Surrey

Christ's Hospital to Guildford

A class D1 tank locomotive pulls pre-bogie type coaches at Rudgwick station on the Christ's Hospital to Guildford line, c1890. (Lens of Sutton)

First ideas for a branch line from Christ's Hospital to Guildford in Surrey came in 1857 at a time when Jacomb Hood, engineer for the LBSCR, was very much involved in battles over a line from Christ's Hospital to Shoreham (chapter 3). Despite his preoccupation, Jacomb Hood saw that such a route would open up possibilities for connections between the South Coast resorts and the Midlands.

A company called the Horsham and Guildford Direct Railway was formed and plans were authorised by Parliament on 6th August 1860. It was agreed the line should be built as single track leaving the Horsham to Pulborough line at Christ's

Hospital. A triangular junction was to be built at this point to allow through running from Brighton to Guildford as well as Horsham to Guildford.

There were many construction problems and at one stage the contractor went bankrupt with a loss of over £30,000. The line was taken over in an incomplete state in 1864 by the LBSCR and work was not finished until the following year. Even at this stage the government inspector would not accept the siting of Rudgwick station on a 1 in 80 gradient and insisted this should be reduced to 1 in 130. Because of this the bridge over the River Arun, south of the station, had to be rebuilt.

Services began on 2nd October 1865 even though Rudgwick station was not finished due to the resiting problem until almost two months later. Initially eight trains ran daily with certain trains terminating at Cranleigh. But the railway authorities had been over-optimistic and traffic was not good. Fares were increased within 18 months of the line's opening.

The triangular junction at Christ's Hospital also ran into difficulties. Intended for through trains to the Midlands, it was not regularly used and the LBSCR closed it within two years. This was probably because they were concerned that their 'old enemies', the LSWR, would have greater access to the South Coast with running powers on this section. No sign of this line remains today with the area ploughed over.

The Guildford line left the main Horsham to Pulborough line at Stammerham junction. Initially there was no station at Stammerham, only a small wooden platform used by a dairy to ferry milk up to London. But the dairy overspent and went bankrupt. The estate was quickly bought at a knock-down price by the Governors of Christ's Hospital School who were anxious to get away from the smoke and grime of London.

When the school arrived in 1902, the LBSCR hoped to encourage residential development in the area. With this in mind, a magnificent brick-built station was erected at a cost of £30,000 and the railway company waited for a 'boom town' to arrive. Seven facing platforms were constructed to deal with five through-tracks. Lines already existed to give trains from

Christ's Hospital station which serves the nearby Bluecoat school seen here in LBSCR days. The station was built to a fine standard in anticipation of a 'boom town' which never arrived. (Lens of Sutton)

London, via Horsham, the option of routes to Pulborough or Shoreham-by-Sea. With Guildford within reach, Christ's Hospital station was set to become an important railway junction serving much of West Sussex. Three platforms covered the branch line to Guildford. On the main line two platforms dealt with passengers and a loop swung off to two facing platforms covering the school passengers and baggage.

Unhappily for the railway authorities the housing development did not occur. It was possibly the arrival of the school that stopped any progress. After the school's efforts to get away from the gloom of London, it was considered hardly likely they would welcome suburban growth over the green fields around them.

Throughout its years the line never came up to expectations. Passenger traffic came mostly from Cranleigh in Surrey where a large amount of useful goods traffic used the through sidings. Before 1867 Cranleigh was spelt 'Cranley'. The change was made at the request of the Post Office to avoid confusion with

Crawley in Sussex on badly written envelopes and parcels.

In 1896 there was a development which could have had an effect on the Guildford line. Plans were deposited for a light railway to run between Ockley (south of Holmwood on the Dorking-Horsham line) and Selham (west of Petworth on the line to Midhurst). Connections would have been made at Cranleigh thus creating a useful junction. Nothing materialised and later plans for a link from Holmwood direct to Cranleigh proposed in 1898 also failed.

During the Second World War there were several incidents on the Guildford line. In 1941 a bomb hit the track just north of the Worthing Road bridge outside Horsham. The line was badly damaged and a bus service was provided between Horsham and Christ's Hospital during repairs.

On 16th December 1942 a German plane strafed and bombed a train at Bramley. There were 42 passengers on the train and a

A damaged passenger train at Bramley which was bombed during the Second World War. (Branch lines to Horsham – Middleton Press)

number were killed and the remainder were admitted to hospital. Fortunately help was immediately forthcoming, including from a number of Canadian soldiers, otherwise things might have been far worse.

On a less serious occasion a locomotive from Pulborough steamed through Christ's Hospital towards Horsham without a driver. A cleaner managed to climb aboard just before Horsham. He had no doubt been surprised to see an engine approaching with several sets of level crossing gates adorning the front buffers and no driver!

The 1955 railway strike sealed the fate of the line to Guildford. All services ceased during the strike and freight traffic never returned to its previous level. The line was now losing money. At the same time, the railways were not helping themselves. Trains were leaving Horsham a few minutes before possible connections, yet there was a 15 minute wait at Cranleigh. The line had outlived its usefulness and when closure proposals were announced in 1963 they came as no surprise. An inquiry was held at Cranleigh Village Hall but protests against the closure were minimal. With such a poor service so little used there was no hope.

The last train left Guildford on 14th July 1965 at 6.55 pm and returned at 8.34 pm. Boys from Christ's Hospital school sang *Abide with Me* to mark the event as the train pulled out. The day after official closure a special train organised by the Locomotive Club of Great Britain covered the entire route. Among the passengers was Bert Andrews, the last Cranleigh signalman, who was the great-grandson of the guard on the first train.

The present Christ's Hospital station bears no resemblance to the grand building of the past. It looks more like a wayside halt and serves one double track only, being the line between Horsham and Pulborough. Gone are the sidings and the school loop line. The platforms on the Guildford line have gone, the area lost in undergrowth. Christ's Hospital station itself was for a time under threat of closure but an outcry from the school plus a petition with 3,046 names sent to the Queen saved the day.

Two and a half miles to the north-west stood Slinfold station.

Christ's Hospital station is today in a much reduced state. Access to the former Christ's Hospital to Guildford line could be gained through where today appears a gap in the trees. (Author)

Slinfold consisted of a single station building with a well-built station house attached. There was no passing loop but, until closure to freight traffic in 1962, a signal box acted as a ground frame for the sidings. (Lens of Sutton)

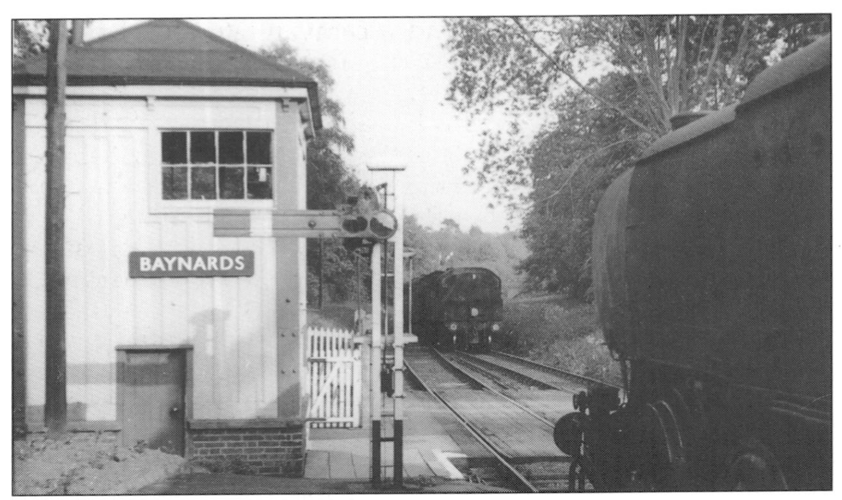

Locomotives 41327 and 33034 pass at Baynards in May 1963. The station was named after nearby Baynards Park. It had a goods yard and a siding to a Fuller's earth plant. (R.K. Blencowe)

The 'Midhurst Belle Special' organised by RCTS/LCGB hauled by USA 0-6-0 tank locomotive 30064 stops briefly at Baynards on 18th October 1964. This locomotive arrived at the Bluebell Railway in October 1971. (R.K. Blencowe)

Today the station has gone and a caravan site took its place. Nearby two LBSCR houses remain on the far side of a former level crossing. Rudgwick station on the Surrey-Sussex border stood south of the village. This has also been demolished and a health centre stands on the site of the station buildings. Between Rudgwick and Baynards was Baynards Tunnel where a summit was reached. Gone now are the days when many freight trains were brought to a halt by the very wet and slippery conditions in the tunnel. Once even a goods train hauled by a powerful Q1 0-6-0 was halted by the incline and conditions.

Baynards station in Surrey was named after the nearby Baynards Park. It had a goods yard and a private siding serving a Fuller's earth plant. The platforms have survived the many years with the station building becoming a private residence. After Cranleigh came Bramley. The bridge over the River Wey has gone and beyond the line joined the Guildford to Portsmouth main line at Peasmarsh. Today most of the trackbed forms part of the Downs Link, a 30 mile long footpath and bridleway linking the North and South Downs.

If one stands long enough on the Guildford line remains of Christ's Hospital station at night, it is perhaps possible to imagine the whistle of a steam train in the distance. Or maybe it is an owl or a fox expressing its pleasure that the 'boom town' did not happen.

6
Along The Upper Medway Valley

East Grinstead to Tunbridge Wells
Spa Valley Railway

Ex-LBSCR B4 4-4-0 locomotive no 2058 arrives at Groombridge in the early 1930s. (Lens of Sutton)

East Grinstead to Tunbridge Wells

A line which opened eastwards from East Grinstead to Tunbridge Wells on 1st October 1866 did much to strengthen the LBSCR's hold on its eastern flank. Two years later another line reached Tunbridge Wells from Uckfield meeting the East

Grinstead line at Groombridge. The LBSCR's hold on the area was now virtually complete.

Various ideas to cover the area had previously been considered. The South Eastern Railway (SER), a bitter rival of the LBSCR, had proposed a line from near Tonbridge to East Grinstead in 1845 but this did not materialise. Other ideas to connect Tunbridge Wells with Lewes and Brighton also failed against LBSCR pressures.

The East Grinstead, Groombridge and Tunbridge Wells company was incorporated in 1862 and an Act was given Royal approval on 7th August 1862. In 1864, while the line was being built, the company was taken over by the LBSCR. The line was single track which was an indication of the amount of traffic anticipated. Known as the Upper Medway Valley line, there were intermediate stations at Forest Row, Hartfield, Withyham and Groombridge. Of the nine trains already running daily from Three Bridges to East Grinstead a number of these were eventually extended to Tunbridge Wells but service levels increased very slowly.

When the Uckfield line opened two years later in 1868, trains from Lewes and Uckfield could only reach East Grinstead by reversing at Groombridge. So in 1878 authority was given for a single track spur to be constructed south from Ashurst junction so that Groombridge could be bypassed. At first it remained unused but it came into its own when the Oxted to Groombridge service opened in 1888. Eventually the spur doubled carrying regular services southwards to Uckfield as well as down the 'Cuckoo Line' to Polegate and Eastbourne (see chapter 7).

East Grinstead station had originally been a terminus, being the end of the line from Three Bridges which opened in 1855. When the Tunbridge Wells line opened a resiting was necessary at East Grinstead to accommodate the track. A new station was built north of the original site, the latter became part of a goods yard and the old station building became a private dwelling. The railway from East Grinstead towards Forest Row skirted the town in deep cuttings and short tunnels under College Road

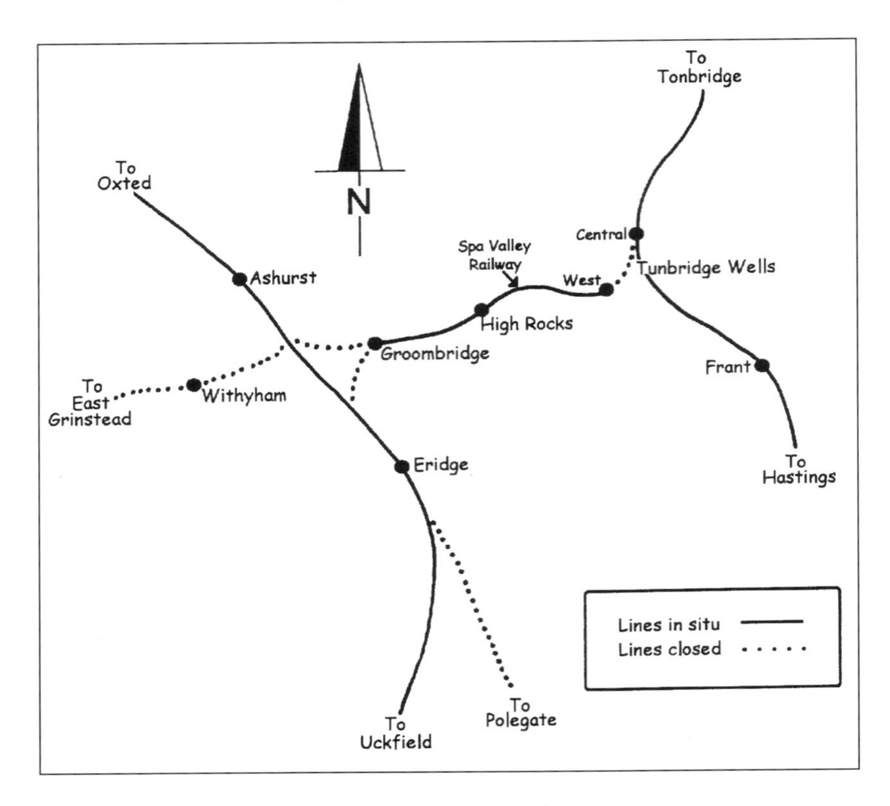

and the A22 Lewes road. Today, with the track long since gone, it has been turned into a road which bypasses the town and has been called (rather unkindly) Beeching Way. The line followed a fairly steep gradient down to Forest Row, some 3¼ miles to the east and into the Medway Valley. Forest Row was a large but fairly scattered village and the station, as happened all too frequently, was inconveniently sited. But this was one of the busier places on the route and often during its life trains carrying commuter traffic from London would be terminated at this station.

The bridge over the A22, just prior to reaching Forest Row station, has been demolished but embankments remain on

Forest Row was one of the busier stations on the East Grinstead to Tunbridge Wells West branch. It closed under the Beeching Axe in 1967 with the site becoming a social club. (Lens of Sutton)

either side. The station itself has long since gone and the area is now in industrial use. Forest Row stands on an old turnpike road which dates back to 1752. South of the village the old coach road split at Witch Cross (now spelt Wych Cross). One fork led to Chailey and Marling Gate (now spelt Malling) at Lewes. The other crossed south-east through Ashdown Forest towards Uckfield along the present A22. A later turnpike road, dated 1766, was established along the present B2110 on to Hartfield and beyond, more or less along the route the railway was to take in later years.

Three and a half miles further east was Hartfield station, situated at a point where the B2026 crossed the B2110. This was A. A. Milne's *Winnie-the-Pooh* territory where Pooh's adventures by sandy banks and streams may well have came to life for many travellers to the village. Part of the station building, to be found on the B2026 road to Edenbridge, has become a nursery school and when visited by the author in September 2000 it was thriving with many enthusiastic young children. As they played

Hartfield station opened in October 1866. In its later years it was used by many visitors to A. A. Milne's 'Winnie-the- Pooh' territory. (Lens of Sutton)

Hartfield station building has become a play school as well as a private dwelling. The station closed to passengers in January 1967. (Author)

on the former platform one wondered how many were aware this was once quite a busy station.

Withyham station has become a private dwelling, hidden behind a high hedge just out of the village. As at a number of other stations along the line, there was no crossing loop but a level crossing existed to the west of the station. Close by the old trackbed is clearly defined. It can be argued that neither Hartfield nor Withyham justified a station but both were required under Section 21 of the Act agreeing the building of the line. Also in pursuance of the Act a siding was to be maintained at Withyham for the private use of Earl Delaware.

Between Withyham and Tunbridge Wells West were (and still are) Groombridge station and High Rocks Halt which until 1985 were served by DEMUs between Eridge and Tonbridge. Today Groombridge and High Rocks Halt are served by the Spa Valley Railway (see end of this chapter).

When the LBSCR built Tunbridge Wells West station it set out

Tunbridge Wells West station was intended as a terminus for LBSCR trains but on its opening it was linked by single track through a tunnel with Tunbridge Wells Central's SER lines. (Lens of Sutton)

D3 class locomotive 0-4-4T no 2386 awaits departure from Tunbridge Wells West bound for Eastbourne on 22nd May 1948. (John H. Meredith)

to impress the local inhabitants. The buildings were indeed quite impressive, embellished with a clock tower, a minor Big Ben, surrounded by a louvred spirelet with a weather vane. The Carlton Hotel was built at the station's side and just beyond it a notice serving to outbid the rival SER read 'London, Brighton & South Coast Railway. New Route to London: Shortest, Quickest and Most Direct. Frequent Express Trains'. The station building is still there today but in commercial use.

On 2nd January 1967 the whole route from Three Bridges to Groombridge fell under the Beeching Axe. The railway authorities could no longer afford to provide a service for the villages along Worth Way and the Upper Medway Valley. The last train ran exactly 100 years and 3 months after its opening. Much of the trackbed between Three Bridges and Groombridge has become a walkway (there are clear footpath signs to which one must adhere).

After closure of the Three Bridges to Groombridge line, 3-

An LBSCR 'balloon' coach at High Rocks, c1910. High Rocks station opened in 1907. After closure in 1952 it reopened in 1998. The Spa Valley Railway's ambition is to extend services to Eridge. (Lens of Sutton)

coach DEMUs ran on a shuttle service between Eridge and Tonbridge via Groombridge and Tunbridge Wells. After Groombridge the line continued to High Rocks Halt (opened in 1907) and Tunbridge Wells West, then on through Tunbridge Wells Central to terminate at Tonbridge. The service finally ceased on 6th July 1985. In earlier years Groombridge, close to the Sussex/Kent border, was a busy station serving four directions but towards the end only sparse traffic existed. Small wonder the line met its doom.

Spa Valley Railway

Despite earlier closures, a railway returned between Groombridge and Tunbridge Wells in 1996 when a preservation society acquired the line. After much hard work a service became available to the public in the same year to be known as the Spa Valley Line which produced a regular service

The Spa Valley Railway operates frequent services between Groombridge and Tunbridge Wells during the summer and on bank holidays and certain weekends. A steam train runs beyond Groombridge so the locomotive may run round the coaches prior to return. (Author)

The 0-6-0 ST steam locomotive 'Fonmon' plus coaches await departure from Groombridge station. The original Groombridge station has become offices and this nearby platform has been built by the Spa Valley Railway. (Author)

throughout the summer and bank holiday periods. Initially trains ran for half a mile out of Tunbridge Wells West but this was extended to Groombridge in August 1997.

The engine shed at Tunbridge Wells West retains its original LBSCR 1891 design and today houses many railway exhibits plus a souvenir shop. The society has acquired many locomotives, steam and diesel, plus numerous items of rolling stock. On the day of the author's visit and despite poor weather, the steam locomotive in use was 0-6-0ST *Fonmon,* built by Peckett in 1924, and the coaches were well laden with passengers.

Apart from numerous special events during the year, the 3 mile line is well worth a visit. Trains can be boarded at Tunbridge Wells West, High Rocks or at Groombridge. The Spa Valley Line's ambition is to extend services to Eridge which would connect with the Uckfield line.

7
The Cuckoo Line

Polegate to Eridge

Hellingly station on the Cuckoo Line. The line to the left to Hellingly Hospital was electrified with overhead wires in 1903. (Lens of Sutton)

The 'Cuckoo Line' from Polegate to Eridge was completed in two stages. The first section, owned by the Tunbridge Wells & Eastbourne Railway Company, opened from Polegate to Hailsham on 14th May 1849. At the same time a line opened southwards from Polegate to Eastbourne. Both lines connected with a route between Brighton, Lewes, Polegate and St Leonards which had opened three years earlier.

The remainder of the route northwards from Hailsham to Eridge was completed 31 years later. The section was approved per an Act dated 1873 initially as a 3 ft gauge line promoted by local businessmen but the scheme developed into a standard gauge system. It opened in stages during 1880. At Eridge the line joined a route opened in 1868 from Uckfield to Groombridge giving both lines through routes to Tunbridge Wells and London via the Oxted line. During construction of the Hailsham to Eridge section, in 1876, the whole line from Eastbourne to Tunbridge Wells was taken over by the LBSCR.

The original Polegate station on the Lewes to St Leonards line stood immediately east of the High Street level crossing. Prior to the railways, Polegate had been an area of little significance being part of the parish of Hailsham. The rail connections that followed to Hailsham and Eastbourne caused the town to grow in importance. The initial route from Eastbourne to Hailsham required a reversal at Polegate and to overcome this a new station was built in Station Road in 1881. Thus Polegate became an important junction and the number of platforms and sidings was increased accordingly.

A train leaves Polegate station, June 1966, for Eastbourne. Polegate station was moved to its present site in 1881 to avoid reversal of Hailsham to Eastbourne trains. (John H. Meredith)

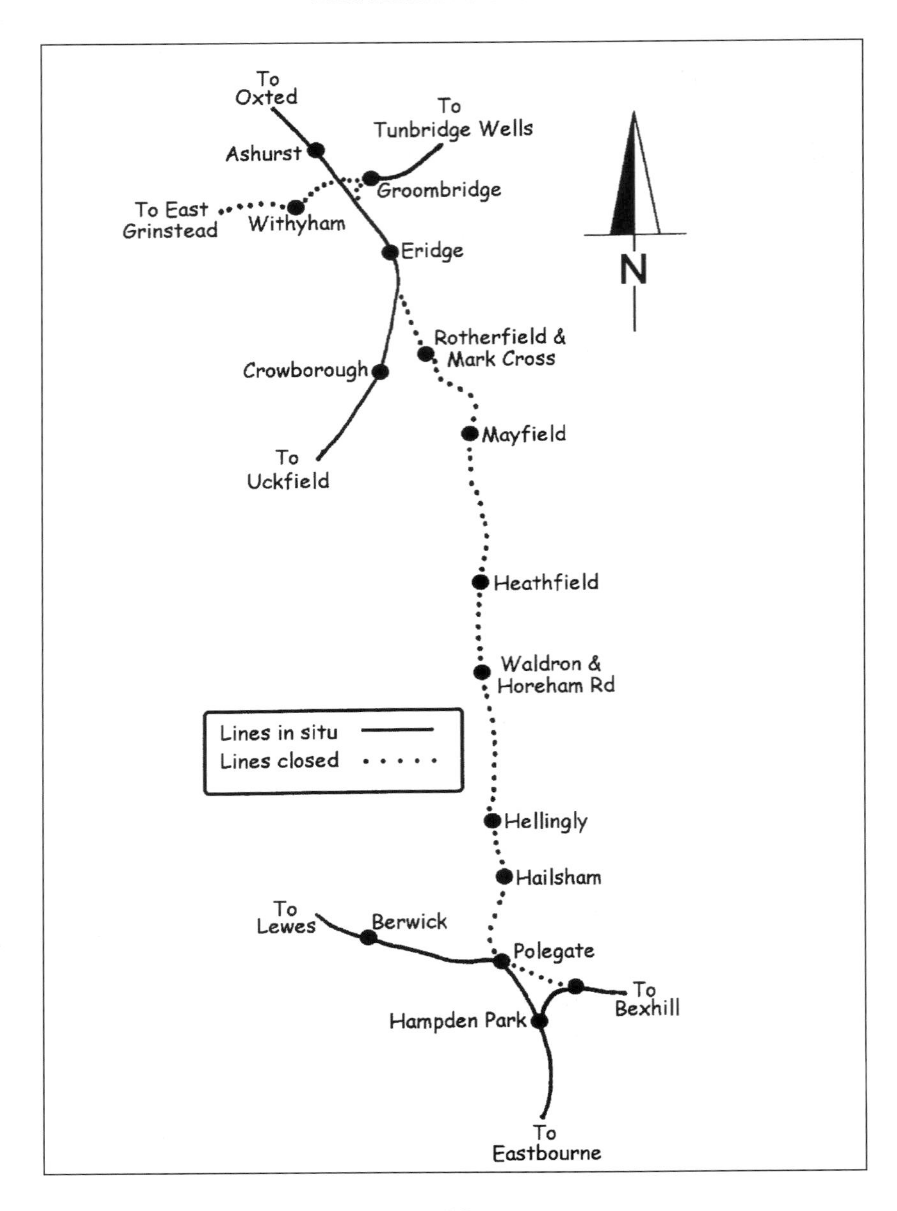
To
Oxted
To
Tunbridge Wells
Ashurst
Groombridge
To East
Grinstead
Withyham
Eridge
N
Rotherfield &
Mark Cross
Crowborough
Mayfield
To
Uckfield
Heathfield
Waldron &
Horeham Rd
Lines in situ
Lines closed
Hellingly
Hailsham
To
Lewes
Berwick
Polegate
To
Bexhill
Hampden Park
To
Eastbourne

Whilst in the Polegate area, it is worth considering another former of transport. For many years, a large brick-faced shed in Coppice Avenue was involved with airships. Built during the First World War it was an airship repair shop. The building was demolished in May 1996 to make way for sheltered homes. But remains of these earlier days still exist for under the Downs at Donkey Hollow traces of airship mooring posts can still be found set into the soil. Before exploring the area, though, ask the farmer's permission since the land is private.

The Polegate airship station was served by the Royal Naval Air Service which selected the site in 1914. By July 1915 one small airship was in commission and two years later Polegate was using the SS (Submarine Scout) Zero type. Much fine work was carried out by them convoying shipping in the Channel including the harassment of enemy submarines.

Back to the Cuckoo Line, the track left Polegate station westwards then northwards along what is now a railway-owned footpath, under the A27 and then along what has

Hailsham station was a terminus from 1849 to 1880. The name of this public house close to the former station is a reminder. (Author)

become Westfield Close. Three miles further north came Hailsham station. As already indicated, Hailsham was a terminus from 1849 to 1880 and this is evidenced by the public house called The Terminus close to the station site. The station itself was a grand affair in the town, comprising two substantial platforms with buildings and many sidings. A private siding served a brickworks 1½ miles to the south of Hailsham near Nightingale Farm.

Hailsham has for many years been a town of some note. In the mid 18th century it was a central point serving numerous turnpike roads in various directions. When the railways came, the turnpike trusts, through competition, corruption and inefficiency, went bankrupt. At the end of the 19th century many of those remaining were taken over by the newly created County Councils. In competition there was a plan put forward to make the River Cuckmere navigable as a canal reaching Hailsham and possibly beyond. But this did not prove practicable and funds were not forthcoming so the idea was dropped.

Locomotive 42101 class 4MT 2-6-4T hauling a Tunbridge Wells to Eastbourne train approaches Hellingly station, October 1955 (John H. Meredith)

Hellingly station and goods yard, October 1950. To the right can be seen the electrified line to Hellingly Hospital plus overhead wiring. The line was abandoned in 1959. (John H. Meredith)

In March 1959 an enthusiasts' special was run to Hellingly Hospital using an electric locomotive and a brake waggon borrowed from BR. (Lens of Sutton)

No doubt the railway at Hailsham assisted in the transport of the town's main trade of the day, this being the manufacture of rope, twine and sacking. Rope has continued to be made locally though lately for a less gruesome purpose than that previously of supplying cords to be used for executions in prisons!

To the north of Hailsham lies the village of Hellingly. The railway station was just south of an overbridge and not far from the magnificently timbered Horselunges Manor built around 1475. The station still exists and it is privately owned. Just south of the station a siding led to nearby Hellingly Mental Hospital. It had no connection with the LBSCR except that a small wooden platform was constructed without a canopy opposite the main (and only) platform.

The railway was used to convey building material, stores and so forth to the hospital and occasionally visitors and staff. For the latter there was a 12-seater four-wheeled tramcar which after closure stood for many years as a pavilion on the hospital sports ground. In 1903 the mile-length line was electrified using the hospital's own generated current at 500 volts DC. The wire was suspended from brackets supported by metal poles spaced out alongside the track. The line closed to passenger traffic in 1931 and the platform was removed in 1932. By 1954 goods traffic was down to about one a day but the line lingered on until March 1959 when it was finally abandoned. On 4th March 1959 a 'special' was run for enthusiasts using the electric locomotive and a brake van borrowed from British Railways.

Just over 3½ miles further north was a station called Horeham Road & Waldron. It served Waldron, 2½ miles away and nearby Horeham Manor. During its life the station had numerous name changes. After the Second World War a settlement developed round the station and the Southern Railway decided on a final name, Horam. After closure, it remained complete but dilapidated for a long time. The goods yard was used by a local coal merchant. Today a nameboard recalling the past stands on a short section of surviving platform.

Heathfield station served a large and scattered village mostly on higher ground. Much of the 2½ mile stretch from Horam to

Heathfield station building is today in commercial use. The station closed to passengers in 1965. (Author)

Heathfield can be walked where footpath signs indicate. It is easily accessible from the B2203 along most of its route. The station at Heathfield and the large goods yard have given way to new buildings but the station building remains in private use. From an overbridge in nearby Station Approach can be seen the south portal of a short tunnel (270 yards) that carried the track under the A265 High Street. It was at the entrance to this tunnel that exciting developments occurred in 1895 when the country's first natural gas deposits were found.

Records have it that first such indications came from the nearby Heathfield Hotel during a search for water. But the hotel did not pursue its find and it was not until the following year that the railway company, extending a bore tube in search of water, found at 312 feet deep a smell of gas. At first it was thought to be foul air but when someone daringly applied a light to the top of the tube there was a huge burst of flame which was extinguished only with considerable difficulty!

A pressure of 140 lbs to the square inch was found to exist and it persisted for about six years. The railway quickly put the gas to good use by illuminating the station. In 1901 some

Beyond the water tank at Heathfield can be seen gas tanks which towards the end of the 19th century contained quantities of the country's first natural gas deposits. (Lens of Sutton)

The entrance to the 270 yard tunnel at Heathfield is close to where natural gas deposits were stored from 1895. (Author)

Americans, under the name of 'The Natural Gas Fields of England Ltd', sank further bore holes, one reaching a depth of 400 ft. The output of one of these was recorded at 15 million cubic feet a day – equivalent in those days to one eighth of the total daily sale of gas in London.

Due to its purity the gas was found to be of great value in research in aid of safety in mines and bottled supplies were taken. By 1934 the gas supply had run out for all practical purposes and the station lighting was converted to use ordinary town gas. From Heathfield trains travelled across open country through woodland and over the River Rother to Mayfield. This was a little used station but a private siding to a milk depot operated until about 1950. The station, which stood about half a mile from the village centre, has been converted to a private house.

After Mayfield the line passed over Rotherfield Lane and then

Mayfield station was a little used station but a private siding to a milk depot operated until the 1950s. After closure of the line in June 1965 the station building became a private residence. (Lens of Sutton)

criss-crossed the A267 in two short tunnels of 60 yds and 70 yds. Rotherfield and Mark Cross lay 2½ miles to the north. Originally Rotherfield was served by a station on the Uckfield line which had opened earlier in 1868. But when the Eridge to Hailsham line came into operation, the original Rotherfield was renamed Crowborough and Jarvis Brook and the Eridge line station took the name, being closer to the villages it served.

When the station was closed it was put to good use as a private dwelling. The platforms were used as sides to a swimming pool and the platform awning was made into a roof for a sun lounge. Today the area has been converted to become a water garden. Near the station site today is the 'Cuckoo Line Stores', reminding shoppers of the former line's identity.

From Rotherfield the track passed down a fairly steep gradient through further wooded countryside to Redgate Mill junction where it joined the line from Uckfield. A single track ran parallel to the Uckfield line along a one and a half mile

Eridge station in pre-motoring times. This was once an important junction with lines to Eastbourne, Lewes, East Grinstead and Tunbridge Wells. (Lens of Sutton)

Eridge station in steam days when it had four facing platforms and sidings. (Lens of Sutton)

Eridge station today which carries a line to Uckfield. On the left, the overgrown bay which once served trains to Tunbridge Wells West. (Author)

Trains pass at Hailsham station not long before closure of the line to passengers in 1965. Freight traffic survived a further 3 years. (R.K. Blencowe)

Under the roadbridge at the former Heathfield station these locomotive wheels serve as a reminder of the past. (Author)

valley towards Eridge. This stretch was incorporated as double track in 1894 to facilitate easier working.

Eridge, a station in remote countryside, came about for the inhabitants of Eridge Castle. It was built as a fine junction with four facing platforms plus sidings anticipating the increase of traffic to follow. But this did not happen and although it still exists today serving the Uckfield line it is still little used. The section of platform that was used by the Cuckoo Line has long since lost its track and only weeds cover the trackbed down to Redgate Mill.

The Cuckoo Line was closed to passengers north of Hailsham on 14th June 1965. Freight trains continued from Hailsham to Heathfield until 26th April 1968 when a bridge became damaged and repair was considered uneconomic and not carried out. Hailsham closed completely on 9th September 1968 and with this the last stretch of the line to Polegate had gone.

The name 'Cuckoo' for the line was adopted by the railwaymen themselves. This relates to the old Sussex legend

A section of Horam's platform still exists under the A267. The station is recalled by the notice on a platform nameboard. (Author)

that on the 14th April annually the first cuckoo of summer is released. Story has it that throughout the winter the cuckoos are all in the keeping of an old woman of somewhat uncertain temper. If she is in a good mood she goes to Heathfield Fair with a cuckoo in her apron, or in a basket, and she releases it there. From that date cuckoos are said to be heard calling all over Sussex.

8
A Racecourse And A Tramway

Midhurst to Chichester
The Selsey Tramway

Ex-LSWR Drummond class M7 0-4-4T locomotive no 256 arrives with a passenger set at Midhurst station in the 1930s. The station closed to regular traffic in 1955. (Lens of Sutton)

Midhurst to Chichester

Heavy earthworks were needed when the LBSCR built a line from Midhurst to Chichester with difficult engineering and steep gradients needed through the South Downs. The line was approved by Parliament in 1876 but did not open until 11th July 1881. It was a costly undertaking necessitating tunnels at Cocking (738 yards), Singleton (741 yards) and West Dean (445

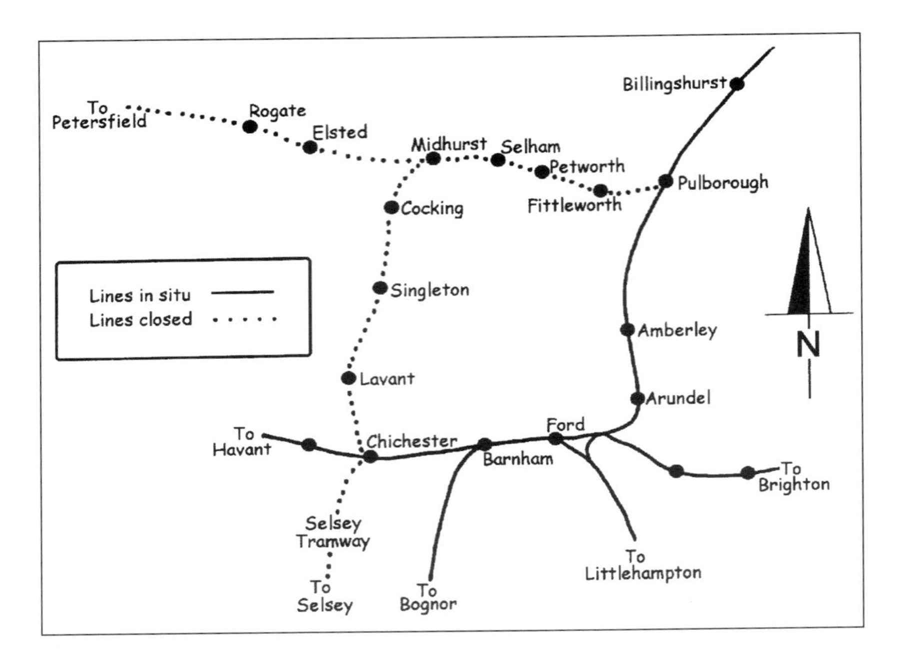

yards). They were built to take double track but the amount of traffic never justified this. There were three intermediate stations, these being Cocking, Singleton and Lavant.

Travelling westwards from Midhurst the line swept in a wide arc southwards. The track ran more or less parallel to the present A286 and after nearly 2½ miles the village of Cocking was reached at the foot of the Downs. After cuttings and tunnels came Singleton, some 3 miles further south.

Singleton was a station of some importance and comprised two island platforms with substantial canopies to cater for the considerable traffic to nearby Goodwood races. The station building was constructed in splendid style and ¾ mile of sidings could hold 14 trains on race days.

'Glorious Goodwood' as it was known was not only one of the major events in Britain's horse racing calendar but a grand social occasion as well. It became all the more desirable when the Prince of Wales, the future Edward VII, abandoned the top hat and tails for the informal panama hat and lounge suit. It was also Edward VII who once described Goodwood as a garden party with racing thrown in.

In these earlier times during summer days trains would bring thousands of race-goers who would then be seen snaking across the Downs along a path towards the racecourse in an endless line. For the gentry there was West Dean House (now West Dean College) where they would gather before and after.

Lavant station was 3 miles further south which for many years served as a railhead for sugar beet. The line finally joined the Chichester to Havant line at Fishbourne Crossing, just under a mile west of Chichester itself. By the 1930s the route fell into decline suffering mostly from bus competition. Rail traffic had been limited for many years and in July 1935 the line was closed to passenger traffic.

During the Second World War the line, like many others, was under frequent attack since it had access to the coast and was

Lavant station on the Midhurst to Chichester line which for many years served as a railhead for sugar beet. (Lens of Sutton)

relatively close to Portsmouth. The tunnels served a useful purpose for the storage of ammunition trains which could be kept out of sight and away from attack.

Freight working north of Lavant ceased in 1953 but the Lavant to Chichester section remained open for seasonal sugar beet traffic. This closed in 1972 after which time the line ended at a gravel pit about half a mile to the south of the station.

Tracing the old line today much of the land is private although it is possible to walk many sections. The tunnels remain and serve various purposes including mushroom growing. A new estate covers most of the approach to Midhurst

Lavant station building has been converted into flats with the forecourt and the yard becoming a housing estate. The former freight track from Chichester to Lavant has been removed with the trackbed becoming a foot/cycle path. (Author)

and part of the trackbed now forms Holmbush Way which leads into New Road. The 1881 Midhurst station has gone, also covered by new development, and The Fairway has been built along the line to the tunnel east of the station.

The first stop south from Midhurst was Cocking. This was an opulent structure with mock timber-framing as a finish. It was a single platform station and there was no crossing loop. There was a small yard to the south. The platform building is now privately owned and the platform edge forms part of an extensive garden. Over a former station entrance a plaque states 'LB&SCR 1880'.

Singleton to the south has retained its station buildings but the platforms are totally overgrown. The goods shed survives in use as a vehicle repair, reclamation and spares organisation. The station building is today privately owned but for a time after

After closure Singleton station building became a vineyard and winery but this has gone and it is today a private residence. During steam days, Singleton had ¾ mile of sidings which catered for trains on race days at nearby Goodwood. (Author)

Cocking station which opened in 1881. Since closure to passengers services in 1935 and goods traffic in 1953 the station building has become a private residence with the platform remaining intact. (Lens of Sutton)

On the former station building at Cocking a plaque showing 'LB&SCR' and 'A.D. 1880' remains as a reminder of the past. (Author)

closure the area became a vineyard with a winery housed in the old booking hall and waiting rooms. It was claimed that the Goodwood lavatory block (used during race days) could store up to 40,000 bottles of wine! History was repeating itself since it is thought that the Romans grew vines at nearby Charlton.

Lavant station building still exists and has become flats. The forecourt and yard are now a select housing estate. The nearby road still crosses by bridge and the former trackbed underneath can be determined. The freight track between Chichester and the Lavant area was pulled up just before privatisation and has become a foot and cycle path.

Following closure of the Midhurst to Chichester line attempts were made to establish a Railway Preservation Society but this failed in 1994 partly since the Edward James Foundation at West Dean did not wish trains to cross the estate. At Chichester many patrons at the Smith & Western restaurant may be unaware that they are eating in what was once a goods shed built in 1881 and customers at Waitrose that they are shopping in a superstore built on a former trackbed.

The Selsey Tramway

The Hundred of Manhood & Selsey Tramway covered a 7½ mile stretch southwards from Chichester across Selsey Bill peninsula and later a further mile to Selsey beach. It was authorised by an Act dated 29th April 1896 and was owned by the Hundred of Manhood & Selsey Tramway Company. It was a comparatively easy line to construct across flat land and it opened on 27th August 1897.

There were five locomotives, the first being *Selsey* which was a Peckett 2-4-2T built for the opening of the line. There were also two twin Shefflex railcar units similar to those used on the Kent & East Sussex Railway. The coaches were tram-type in appearance, hence the line was known as the Selsey Tramway.

Services began with an opening ceremony at Chichester station. The mayor, after suitable opening speeches, then astonished his audience by saying he would drive the engine on

The 10.30 am mixed freight train from Chichester in 1920 on the Hundred of Manhood & Selsey Tramway hauled by no 2 'Sidlesham' 0-6-0ST Manning Wardle 21 of 1861. (Author's collection)

When economies became necessary in the 1920s railcars were used on the Selsey Tramway. The line went bankrupt in 1931 and closed finally in l935. (Lens of Sutton)

its first journey. Perhaps fortunately for the passengers the driver did not let this happen and only allowed him to step on the footplate and sound the whistle.

It took 30 minutes to reach Selsey Bridge whereupon the passengers proceeded to a celebratory lunch at Beacon House. The mayor made a further speech, presumably reconciled to not being allowed to drive the engine, and spoke of his hopes that the flagging agriculture of the district might now revive. He also hoped people would now go to the seaside at Selsey instead of Bognor where he had always considered the inhabitants somewhat 'stand-offish'!

The number of 'trams' depended upon the season. In summer there were up to twelve a day and in the winter usually six. Most of the stopping places were mere halts. Hunston, Chalder, Sidlesham and Selsey Bridge comprised single platforms with shelters of corrugated iron. Others had no shelter and one was intended for golf-players only.

Hunston station on the Selsey Tramway. Many of the halts on the line were very basic with shelters of corrugated iron. Other halts had no shelter and one was intended for golf-players only. (Lens of Sutton)

In August 1898 an extension of ½ mile to Selsey beach was opened but this was not widely used. It closed in 1904 never to reopen. In 1910 the sea breached the wall at Pagham Harbour and a section of the line was flooded. Unusually, locomotives and rolling stock were at each end of the line that night and a shuttle service was necessary until the embankment could be rebuilt and raised 12 ft.

The railway became bankrupt in 1931. Hopes that it would be taken over by the Southern Railway were in vain and on 19th January 1935 the West Sussex Railway (as it was now called) went out of business. It was sold to a Gloucestershire contractor for £3,610 and within a short time almost every sign of the line had been removed.

In reporting its closure, the *Daily Express* of 21st January 1935 referred to some of the line's more 'unusual' aspects. It said that of the nine stations along the line, none of them had a porter or booking office. Ferry station comprised only a few sleepers tied together for a platform and a small wooden shed for a shelter. In the last two years of its life, the article said, being single track a breakdown meant no more services for the day. So the railway

Passengers leave Selsey station, c1910. The tramway was once referred to as the 'noisiest and most rickety railway in England'. (Lens of Sutton)

Flooding along the Selsey Tramway was a frequent occurrence. In December 1910 the sea wall was breached at Pagham Harbour and the track was flooded. This picture shows a strengthened embankment at Sidlesham. (John H. Meredith)

staff sent a boy along on a bicycle to tell anyone waiting at the stations that there would be no further trains until the next day!

The best reminder of the line today is probably the Selsey Tram public house in Stockbridge Road, Chichester, where the inn sign carries a drawing of a locomotive as used in the past. The track used to pass along the footpath behind the public house and then followed the canal southwards to Hunston and on to Sidlesham.

Beyond Sidlesham the track skirted the edge of the popular Pagham Harbour Nature Reserve well known for the many varieties of bird life. Selsey station has gone but it was sited just north of the Stargazers Hotel near the junction of Manor Road and Elm Tree Close. All traces of the beach extension have gone.

At the turn of the century it was possible to take a train from Midhurst to Selsey beach with only a change at Chichester. It was a leisurely and pleasant journey through the South Downs and then across open farmland combined with delightful views of Pagham Harbour. Today a motorist may hurtle down the busy A286, through the crowded centre of Chichester and then along the B2201, frequently without a sideways glance. Then he may have to find a spot in Selsey to park his car. Oh for the days of steam!

9
The Bluebell Line – Past And Present

Lewes to East Grinstead
The Bluebell Railway

Sheffield Park station showing neglect after closure in 1958. The station is today well known as the headquarters of the Bluebell Railway. (Lens of Sutton)

Lewes to East Grinstead

A steam train hauled by ex-BR 4-6-0 class 5MT locomotive no 73082 *Camelot* built in 1955 pulls into Sheffield Park station. Soon the platform is crowded as many passengers alight, some

Horsted Keynes station viewed from the south, March 1958. Electric unit 1832 awaits departure. The short link via Ardingly was built 'officially' to relieve congestion at Haywards Heath for the local service from Seaford. (John H. Meredith)

with excited children pulling parents along behind them. This scene could have taken place during any summer month in the early 1900s when the railways enjoyed great popularity. Yet it was Saturday, 23rd September 2000 and a train had just pulled in from Horsted Keynes on the restored and popular Bluebell Line.

Today's Bluebell Railway comprises a section of the original Lewes & East Grinstead Railway Company which was formed in 1875. This was to be one of the last major proposals in Sussex which would complete the LBSCR network that was to exist for many years. An Act of Parliament given Royal Approval on 10th August 1877 agreed that construction of the 17 mile stretch from Culver junction (north of Lewes) to East Grinstead could proceed.

Bitterness had continued to rage between the LBSCR and the SER over territory rights in the area. With the line from Three

Bridges to Tunbridge Wells already in existence, the Lewes & East Grinstead Railway had been formed with a view to improving communications between East Grinstead and London to the north and to Lewes, the county town, to the south. The LBSCR was approached but, although interested in a line to Lewes, it could not offer support northwards towards Oxted. This was because it was already considering such an enterprise itself in conjunction with the SER and any direct move would be considered hostile. With complications to the north, the LBSCR-backed Lewes & East Grinstead Railway Company directed its interests towards Lewes.

An Act agreed in 1878 clarified the situation. This confirmed LBSCR/SER joint involvement with the Oxted line and accepted total ownership by the LBSCR of the Lewes line. Another significant clause was Section 35 which was to prove so important many years later. This was an agreement whereby the LBSCR undertook to run four trains daily between East

Barcombe station on the former Lewes to East Grinstead line is today privately owned. The station was first known as New Barcombe. (Author)

Grinstead and Lewes calling at West Hoathly, Horsted Keynes, Fletching & Sheffield Park and Newick & Chailey. It was this act that local residents seized upon in 1956 thus prolonging closure for nearly three years until another Act was agreed.

The line, now under LBSCR control, opened in August 1882. With the 1878 agreement in force, a 'second route' from East Grinstead to Brighton became possible via Horsted Keynes and Haywards Heath in 1883 (see chapter 10). In addition many trains were to use the East Grinstead and Lewes route to Brighton although it was not until 1904 that full use was made of these connections.

The official LBSCR name for the line from East Grinstead to Lewes became the Sheffield Park line. References to the 'Bluebell Line' were first claimed by the popular press in 1958 when a preservation group was being formed to keep open part of the track. Earlier ideas associated the name with a popular legend of passengers who had managed to alight to gather bluebells and then run hard enough to rejoin their slow-moving train.

Leaving the Lewes to Uckfield track at Culver junction, the

Newick & Chailey station earlier last century. The buildings have been demolished and a housing estate has been built on the site. The far bridge carries the A272. (Lens of Sutton)

Class E4 locomotive no 32581 hauls mixed freight at Sheffield Park before final closure to regular traffic. (John H. Meredith)

An RCTS special hauled by ex-LBSCR Billington class D3 0-4-4T locomotive no 32390 at Sheffield Park takes on water. (Lens of Sutton)

first station northwards was at Barcombe. This was opened as New Barcombe when services began but changed to just Barcombe the next year. The original Barcombe was nearby on the Uckfield line and this changed to Barcombe Mills when the East Grinstead line opened. The village was indeed fortunate to have two railway stations less than a mile apart for such a sparse population. The Sheffield Park line station comprised a fairly large building and single platform plus signal box and sidings. Today the station building is privately owned.

From Barcombe the track switch-backed across low hills and through the 63 yard Cinder Hill tunnel 3½ miles northwards to Newick & Chailey. This station has now entirely disappeared, giving way to a residential development along Lower Station Road off the A272 between the two villages. When the railway opened, local schoolchildren were given a day off to join the many who watched the first train arrive. At that time there were many country folk in the villages who had never seen a train, let alone ridden in one, so it was a day of great excitement. The station had up and down platforms to allow trains to pass and,

Staff pose at West Hoathly, c1910. After closure the station buildings were completely demolished. (Lens of Sutton)

The up platform at Kingscote in the 1950s. (Lens of Sutton)

from its day of opening, a licensed refreshment room. In the 1890s a goods yard was provided. By the end of the 19th century it was busy with some 20 trains a day carrying passengers to such places as Lewes and East Grinstead for school and shopping. Freight too was busy carrying milk, fruit, corn and local produce.

Sheffield Park station, a mile or so onward, was originally known as Fletching & Sheffield Park, changing to its present name in 1883. Sheffield Park station was very similar to Newick & Chailey with a station-master's house and two platforms plus a passenger bridge, a signal box at the north end of the down platform and a second at the south end of the up platform controlling a goods yard. The next station northwards was Horsted Keynes. The station buildings were on the down side but the platform there (giving a face each side of the down Lewes line) does not appear to have been used when the station was first opened. Horsted Keynes had (and still has) a yard on the down side south of the station. The line northwards from Horsted Keynes was built as double track.

After a 1 in 75 rise a summit was reached at West Hoathly Tunnel, 731 yards long, quite straight and the longest on a preserved railway. It was notoriously wet and slippery and gave many problems. Coming out of the tunnel into a cutting, the track levelled off for West Hoathly station. It was another fine station with two platforms, signal box and sidings on both sides. A walk up the steep station road leads to West Hoathly and nearby Sharpthorne. This is a typical instance of a station's remoteness from its villages, particularly since West Hoathly is ½ mile and a climb of 220 ft away. West Hoathly station has been demolished although representations are currently being made for it to reopen when the planned extension to East Grinstead is complete.

Beyond West Hoathly the line fell for nearly two miles at around 1 in 125 to reach Kingscote, an isolated station so named after nearby Kingscote House. The station had a sizeable goods

Locomotive 73082 runs round coaches at Sheffield Park on the Bluebell Line prior to the train's return to Kingscote. This ex-BR class 5MT 4-6-0 locomotive named 'Camelot' was built in 1955. (Author)

Kingscote station building in LBSCR days. (Lens of Sutton)

yard on the up side, north of the station, now in use as industrial premises. Etched in a stone over a window to the left of the station building entrance exists the inscription 'LB&SCR 1882'.

Kingscote was described as a station for Turners Hill which was two miles to the west and an important village on the 1770 turnpike road from London to Brighton. Whilst travelling the B2110 from Turners Hill to East Grinstead note the longish road tunnel under the old line near Kingscote which was built to LBSCR specification.

Beyond Kingscote, after passing through a long cutting, trains crossed the 10-arch Imberhorne Viaduct, so named after a nearby estate, to reach East Grinstead's low-level station. East Grinstead station had a yard to the south, also a connecting line (not used by passengers) to reach the high-level yard of the old (1866) station.

After a steady decline in traffic the line officially closed in 1955. A date was set for 17th June 1955 but due to a strike by ASLEF the last train actually ran on the 28th May 1955. But the closure met considerable hostility from the public. Those agitating referred to the 1878 Act (mentioned earlier in this

Much has been done to restore Kingscote to its present fine condition. When visited in September 2000 it was the northern terminus for Bluebell trains and work was in hand to complete an extension to East Grinstead. (Author)

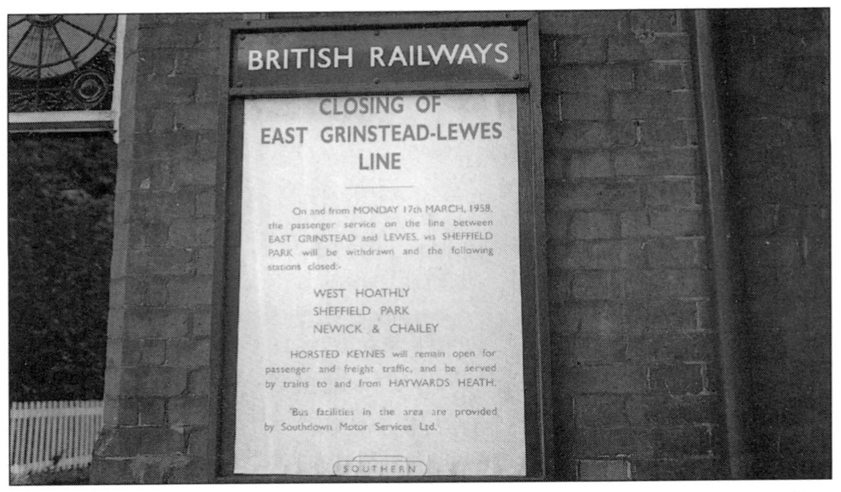

A notice at present-day Kingscote station reminds visitors of the impending closure of the line in March 1958 with trains being replaced by Southdown buses. (Author)

Champagne was used to celebrate the first electric train to reach East Grinstead at the launch of services on the South East Network on 30th September 1987. This service will at a future date connect with Bluebell Railway trains when work between Kingscote and East Grinstead is completed. (Author)

chapter) to invoke a clause in the agreement whereby the LBSCR and the Lewes & East Grinstead Company guaranteed certain stations on the line four trains a day. With this information, BR was forced to reopen from August 1956. Although meeting the law the trains were run at a time when nobody wanted them within an 8 hour shift of locomotive crews. It became known as 'the sulky service'!

This nonsensical situation continued until another Act was agreed and the line closed again on 17th March 1958. This was with the exception of the Horsted Keynes to East Grinstead section which remained on a care and maintenance basis until 1960. But, for part of the line at least, its days were far from over. The track between Sheffield Park and Horsted Keynes was reopened in 1960 by a preservation group and since that time the society has never looked back.

The Bluebell Railway

Today all is activity and the rolling stock to date includes over 30 locomotives of various descriptions, nearly 50 passenger vehicles and more than 30 goods vehicles. The society continues to flourish and platforms crowded with enthusiastic passengers must make today's privatised railways very envious at times! Another important role for the Bluebell is for its use in films and also various BBC and ITV programmes. Carlton TV's *The Railway Children* attracted much publicity when it was shot on location with Jenny Agutter among the cast. Much of the activity, spread over a three week period, was around Horsted Keynes station.

In May 2000 the Bluebell Railway Preservation Society celebrated the 40th anniversary of its beginnings. On 17th May 1960 the society took delivery of its first steam locomotive Terrier no 55 which was to regain its name *Stepney*. The engine, in working order and considered a bargain at £550, arrived with two carriages, nos 320 and 6575 at £100 each. Later during November 2000 a special 125th birthday was held for *Stepney*, the ex-LBSCR class A1X locomotive which was built in 1875.

Kingscote has been splendidly restored and a full service currently runs between Sheffield Park and Kingscote. Work on the extension to East Grinstead continues but this has been hampered by delays over certain land purchases. The removal of rubbish from Imberhorne Lane Tip, deposited over 25 years in a cutting 60 ft deep and ¼ mile long, is also a major factor. Repairs to Imberhorne Viaduct are also necessary plus completion of plans for a Bluebell Railway terminal station at East Grinstead.

When East Grinstead station is reached there will be a physical link with Railtrack metals. This will be of considerable advantage to the Bluebell Railway for delivery of locomotives and rolling stock. In addition the link will certainly encourage excursions to Sheffield Park, requiring only a change of trains at East Grinstead from the electric service which commenced in October 1987. Through working of special trains may also be possible from time to time.

The original line from Three Bridges to East Grinstead was considerably delayed by a landowner in Rowfant in 1855. Whilst repossessing land for its northern extension, the Bluebell Railway can only hope it will be able to overcome the same problems that were experienced in Victorian times!

10
An Alternative Route And A Doomed Railway

Horsted Keynes to Haywards Heath
The Ouse Valley Railway

An electric train service between Horsted Keynes (above) and Haywards Heath (via Ardingly) lasted until October 1963. (Lens of Sutton)

Horsted Keynes to Haywards Heath

The 3½ mile double-track line from Copyhold junction (north of Haywards Heath) to Horsted Keynes lasted almost 80 years. This was a link, leaving the Sheffield Park line some six miles south of

East Grinstead, to join the main line from London to Brighton. Approval to go ahead was given to the LBSCR in July 1880.

The Ardingly line, as it became known, was opened on 3rd September 1883. Although short, considerable structural problems were encountered. There were about eight bridges on the route and this included a six-arch viaduct to cross Sherriffs Mill Road. There was also a tunnel at Lywood, 218 yards long, which took the tracks under the B2028 between Turners Hill and Lindfield. The line crossed the River Ouse just west of Ardingly station, the only station to be built.

The trains used the island platform at Horsted Keynes on the west side before curving westwards down a gradient in parts as steep as 1 in 70. After crossing the six-arch viaduct, the track rose to a small summit beyond which was Lywood Tunnel. Ardingly station came next with a yard behind the down platform. The track from the station rose steeply to Copyhold Cutting where it met the main line 1½ miles north of Haywards Heath. Shortly before this point it crossed the partly-completed route of the Ouse Valley line (covered later in this chapter).

Apart from linking these two important routes, the line served very little additional purpose. Surprisingly it was electrified in 1935 and this was used as a means to reverse trains from Seaford clear of the main line at Haywards Heath. The project would have served greater purpose had the route northwards from Horsted Keynes been similarly electrified and then on through to Croydon. This had been originally planned in the late 1930s but it did not happen. Only as recently as 1987 was the East Grinstead to Croydon line electrified but it was too late. The Horsted Keynes to Haywards Heath link had gone.

Although Ardingly station was built well over a mile from the village, it certainly benefited from Ardingly College only ½ mile away. The school originally existed at Shoreham in Sussex but there was a need to enlarge. It moved to Ardingly in 1870 and 13 years later the railway was opened. In the early part of the last century it is recorded that pupils would arrive at the station by special school trains. The boys, wearing pork pie hats and carrying raincoats, would then march up the hill to the school.

Ardingly station not long before closure of the Horsted Keynes to Haywards Heath branch. During the Second World War the importance of this short link was appreciated. Had the Ouse Valley Viaduct on the London-Brighton line been damaged, it would have provided an alternative route. (Lens of Sutton)

On the platform behind them remained assorted trunks and tuck boxes to be collected later by a farm cart.

After closure of the line, the college retained a firm link with the railway of the past. The nameplate of the 'Schools' class locomotive no 915 *Ardingly* was presented to the college when the engine was withdrawn. Although named after the college, no evidence can be found that the locomotive ever entered Ardingly station.

It was during the 1939-1945 war that the full importance of this short line was appreciated. With the possibility of disruptions on the main line – especially possible damage to the Ouse Valley Viaduct – this alternative route to the coast was kept open. It was covered to the point that, in case of need, the signal box at Horsted Keynes was manned 24 hours a day.

In spite of its potential usefulness, the railway authorities saw fit to close it and the last official train covered the whole route on

Horsted Keynes station not long before closure of the electric service. The platform nameboard states 'Alight here for the Bluebell Line.' (Lens of Sutton)

28th October 1963. When the six-arch Sherriffs Mill Road viaduct was blown up 'for maintenance reasons' at a later date, the last alternative route had gone for good. Only a short section remains, being a single-line track to a railhead for aggregate traffic at Ardingly. The station has been demolished except for one building which is now used as offices.

The surviving section of track to Ardingly which leaves the London to Brighton main line north of Haywards Heath can best be seen from Copyhold Bridge about a hundred yards or so along Copyhold Lane off Bordehill Lane on the Haywards Heath to Balcombe road. The Bluebell Railway has hopes that at some future date the whole Ardingly line might be restored giving a further useful connection to main line metals. But much would need to be done.

Ardingly station building, September 2000. The station was demolished to become a railhead for an aggregate company. (Author)

On the left the London to Brighton line and on the right a freight line to Ardingly photographed from Copyhold Bridge, Haywards Heath. This is also the area where the doomed Ouse Valley Railway was planned. (Author)

The Ouse Valley Railway

On the road between Balcombe and Haywards Heath can be found evidence of an abandoned railway. A sign of a proposed route can just be seen through overgrown bushes at Skew Bridge between Copyhold Lane and the Ouse Valley Railway viaduct. Skew Bridge was built to accommodate the London to Brighton main line but extra wide abutments were added on the east side intended to carry track away from the main line.

The Ouse Valley line was first approved in 1864. It will be recalled from earlier chapters that this was a time when the LBSCR was battling to secure its territory 'rights' in the east. The idea to construct this line was purely political and from the outset it was clear that traffic would be minimal. Work probably began in 1865 on a route that would have taken trains from south of Balcombe along the Ouse Valley to Uckfield and then south east to Hailsham. There it could have connected with a line opened in 1849 from Polegate.

Its object was to counter threatened intrusion by the SER and the LCDR who were planning routes to Eastbourne and Brighton. Fortunately for the LBSCR, which was at that time going through a period of financial difficulties, an 'armistice' was agreed in 1866. As a result all work was brought to a sudden halt. The line would have been expensive with share capital fixed at £280,000.

Beyond Skew Bridge the Ouse Valley line would have crossed above the Ardingly line (to be built 18 years later) and follow a south-easterly route. A stretch of embankment survives today and can be seen to the north of Copyhold Lane. It is quite substantial although incomplete at the western end. No track was ever laid along the route and the embankment has become heavily wooded. Along Copyhold Lane on the left by a kink in the road can be found a partially built road bridge, also much obscured by trees and bushes.

Eastwards from the bridge the line cuts through Wickham Wood to cross High Beech Lane. From here onwards stretches were cut through the countryside and at a private dwelling called Kenwards part of a cutting has been tastefully converted to a private lake surrounded by colourful plants.

North of Lindfield the embankment suddenly stops. The remains cross a public footpath along Spring Lane off the northern end of Lindfield High Street. Lower in the High Street can be seen where the track would have crossed the road and it is reasonable to presume a station would have been built in the area. At the time the earthworks were carried out, local records have it that there was much resistance to a railway through Lindfield but had the railway company persisted no doubt it would have been allowed.

Beyond Lindfield it is not difficult to speculate a route. Following the River Ouse it could have reached Sheffield Park, to be met by the line that was built 16 years later. What possibilities there could have been for the present preservation society with this additional track! From Sheffield Park the line could have continued in a south-westerly direction criss-crossing the Ouse north of Newick with possibly another stop at Piltdown or Shortbridge (perhaps 'Piltdown and Shortbridge' station). Pure speculation of course, but interesting.

Earthworks next appear in the private grounds near Beeches Farm south of Shortbridge, but ask permission if you wish to investigate. Here a deep cutting stops abruptly and possibly a short tunnel had been contemplated. Between Beeches Farm and Owlsbury Farm (approached from the A26 south of Uckfield) flows the River Uck. Further embankments were constructed across this area and clearance of earthworks west of the river proved useful recently. This provided large quantities of soil to help make up the new road junction north of the A272/A275 at North Chailey near the Kings Head.

West of Owlsbury Farm lies the old Lewes to Uckfield trackbed. Walk this track northwards and within ½ mile another embankment will join from the left. This was the final stretch of the doomed Ouse Valley line. Before this is reached the only completed railway bridge on the route can be seen across a field near the winding River Uck.

It might be presumed from this that trains for Hailsham

would leave the Uckfield to Buxted line west of Uckfield to pass through Framfield, East Hoathly, Chiddingly and Lower Horsebridge. Here it could link with the then terminus giving through services to Polegate and Eastbourne.

Certainly quite a direct route could have been available from Three Bridges, through Sheffield Park, Uckfield and Hailsham to the coast. But the spur from Wivelsfield to Polegate via Lewes had already been in existence since 1847 providing a fully adequate service. The Ouse Valley line had been doomed before it even began.

A reminder of the Ouse Valley line can be recalled from the cutting near Beeches Farm south of Shortbridge. It is said that this was part of a strategic defence line during the Second World War and with the area surrounded by tall trees it was thought enemy tanks could be lured into the cutting and be unable to escape. A visitor with more vivid recollections from the war might consider this fanciful. Perhaps it was more likely that one could imagine Captain Mainwaring and his platoon hidden in the undergrowth!

11
Railways Around Brighton And A 'Sea-going' Tramway

The Dyke Railway
The Dyke Steep-Grade Railway
Kemp Town Branch
Volk's 'Daddy Long-Legs' Tramway

An E4 class 0-6-2T no 2494 and 'balloon' coach await clearance at Dyke station in the 1930s before returning to Brighton. (Lens of Sutton)

The Dyke Railway

The Brighton & Dyke Railway Company was approved by Parliament on 2nd August 1877. Various ideas had been submitted before this date. In 1872 it had been suggested a line should be constructed from Preston to the parish of Poynings.

The branch would have terminated 130 yards north-west of the Dyke Hotel in the area of the north-facing slope. The Bill was rejected since Parliament felt that as it would not connect with any main line it would be too isolated.

Next a branch from the main line was considered, from south of Patcham Tunnel again to terminate near the north-facing slope. This was also rejected and next a line from Hove up to Dyke Farm was considered. But difficulties with landowners were experienced and it was not until 1877 that further efforts were made and the proposal finally approved.

The idea was slow to materialise partly due to lack of co-operation from the LBSCR on whose lines the company would have running powers. Eventually, on 1st September 1887, after three extensions to the Act, the first train made the journey of nearly 4 miles to Dyke station. The terminus was about ¼ mile short of the summit and return fares were 2s 6d first class, 1s 8d second class and 1s 3d third class.

A 4-4-2 tank locomotive arrives at Dyke station. The short branch of nearly 4 miles opened in 1887, closing for passengers in January 1939. (Lens of Sutton)

A train arrives at Dyke station, c1910. The branch to the Dyke stopped ¼ mile short of the summit, giving passengers a steep climb ahead. (Lens of Sutton)

The opening ceremony was planned as a splendid affair but the weather determined otherwise. A sumptuous luncheon had been prepared and the band of the 1st Sussex Artillery provided the music, but heavy rain persisted. Eventually the luncheon party took pity on the band and all were invited inside the marquee. It is said the lunch and drinks were accompanied with entertaining speeches with the special guests returning to Brighton on the 5 pm train.

Perhaps better entertained were the railway workers left behind who found a large barrel of beer not drunk. Their toasts to the promoters and shareholders of the Devil's Dyke Railway were apparently much enjoyed and prolonged!

Initially trains ran from West Brighton (now called Hove) direct to Dyke station. But over the years traffic dwindled and halts were opened to encourage further traffic. Golf Club Halt opened in 1891 just short of the terminus. It was a simple brick platform with a nameboard only. No shelter or lighting was provided and passengers would wait in the club house only 50 yards away.

Dyke station is today Dyke Farm. Viewed from above it can be seen how the track snaked its way across the Downs towards West Brighton station (now called Hove). (Author)

In 1895 an agreement was reached whereby the railway authorities installed a bell in the club house which would ring when the starting signal at the Dyke was lowered. In this way golfers had time to finish their drinks and hurry to the platform for the train!

During construction of the line at Golf Club Halt, workers unearthed the skeleton of a woman and around her neck was a string of precious stones. It was said this was the woman who had frightened away the Devil in his attempts during the night to dig through the Downs intending to flood the Weald and its churches. According to legend she placed a lantern in her window and the Devil fled thinking dawn had come. Had her remains been preserved, said a local newspaper, they would have been 'worth their weight in gold to the shareholders'. The report added that many would flock to the Dyke (by train) to look upon the woman who had saved many lives.

In 1905 Dyke Junction Halt was opened. Situated on the Brighton to Worthing line it consisted of two wooden platforms only. In 1932 it was renamed Aldrington Halt. Rowan Halt was added in 1934, half a mile from the junction. This was opened to serve the new Aldrington Manor Estate north of the Old Shoreham Road and was needed to boost flagging trade.

Apart from a temporary closure during the First World War the Dyke Railway, now part of the Southern Railway, closed for good in January 1939. The farm above Dyke station became a target for practice artillery shooting from Ditchling Beacon during the Second World War. Only the foundations were left.

After the war, Dyke station was cleared and the present Dyke Farm took its place. Today Dyke Farm building carries a Crown plaque dated 1949. Not far away cattle graze contentedly where once steam trains puffed their way regularly up the side of the Downs.

Golf Club Halt on the Dyke branch opened in 1891. When a train left the terminus a bell rang in the club house (photographed above – September 2000) to give golfers time to finish their drinks before travelling! (Author)

From 1897 to 1908 a steep-grade railway carried passengers from Poynings up the side of the hill to the Dyke. Nearly a century later the foundations of the engine house can still be found close to the Dyke Hotel. (Author)

The Dyke Steep-Grade Railway

In 1897 a different sort of railway came to the Dyke. It was a steep-grade passenger-carrying railway operated on the north-facing slope between Poynings and the Dyke's summit where earlier a hotel and funfair had been opened. It cost £9,000 to build and the two open-sided cars each carried up to 14 passengers. The railway operated on a cable basis and the cars were driven simultaneously by a 25 bhp oil engine. The gradient of the 840 ft long 3 ft gauge track varied between 1 in 1.5 and 1 in 2.9.

The cars travelled at less than 3 mph and the single fare was 2d. Although initially very popular, the railway did not succeed. It lasted only three years and in December 1900 it was put up for sale but there were no suitable offers so it went for £390. The steep-grade railway lingered on and finally closed in 1908. Its tracks were removed by the end of the First World War. Today

The hillside railway was built by the landlord of the Dyke Hotel and carried passengers up and down the north-facing slope of the Downs at 2d a time. (Author's collection)

the foundations are clearly visible and the upper end platform can be seen only a short distance from the hotel.

Foundations also remain from a cableway that was built across the Dyke ravine earlier in 1894. For the price of 6d passengers could delight in being suspended in mid-air as high as 230 ft from the ground. The cableway was an elaborate affair and the 'stations' were 1,100 ft apart.

Like the steep-grade railway, it was not very successful. The number of 'passengers' steadily declined and by around 1909 the cableway was closed. Destruction was completed during the First World War when the remains were used as target practice for 50 lb bombs.

Kemp Town Branch

The area known as Kemp Town originated in the 1820s when Thomas Kemp set about building a large residential estate to the

Stroudley Terrier no 659 and balloon coach at Kemp Town await their return to Brighton. (Lens of Sutton)

east of Brighton. His intention, he said, was to attract 'fashionable people' out of the already cramped Brighton. But Kemp ran into financial troubles and later he was to work with William Cubitt, one of his leading builders, who later became a prominent railway engineer.

Equally a railway branch to Kemp Town from Brighton proved very costly for such a short distance and comprised almost entirely embankments, viaducts and a 1,024 yard tunnel. It was an undertaking the LBSCR could hardly afford but it was built at a time when the LCDR were pressing for a line to be approved from Beckenham via Lewes to Kemp Town. There were even plans to go into Brighton with a rival terminus to be built opposite the Royal Pavilion! The SER also had ideas for a line from Brighton to Tunbridge Wells which added to the pressure. Bitter fights followed but the LCDR route did not materialise and the SER application also failed.

Approval for the LBSCR to go ahead was obtained on the 13th May 1864 but the branch took over five years to complete.

Services commenced on 2nd August 1869 from Kemp Town junction on the Brighton to Lewes line and curved southwards to just outside Kemp Town itself. Heavy engineering was necessary plus a 14-arch viaduct over Lewes Road similar to the London Road viaduct on the Lewes line. Beyond the viaduct came Lewes Road station which was opened on 1st September 1873. It comprised an island platform with another platform carrying the station buildings. There was a small goods yard. From Lewes Road station the track became single to cross a smaller three-arch viaduct over Hartington Road where a halt by that name opened in 1906.

Finally the track entered the 946 yard Kemp Town Tunnel to emerge almost directly into the terminus. The station had a single platform and quite a range of buildings. It was expected that other platforms would follow but that did not happen. An extensive goods yard was completed in the 1870s but this was not used to expectations. Kemp Town had been considered as a depot to take much of the freight from Brighton but it never succeeded. Even so it continued in use for coal and general goods for many years.

Initially there were nine trips daily increasing to 17 a day by 1883 and 32 daily by 1906. For a time a railcar was used but this was soon replaced by the push and pull 3rd class 'balloon' type coach with an 0-4-2 tank locomotive.

In 1886 the Brighton, Rottingdean & Newhaven Direct Railway received Royal Assent to construct a line starting from Kemp Town station with a route along the coastal area. It was to cross the River Ouse by an opening bridge at Newhaven to join an existing line to Seaford. Despite various extensions to the Act until 1892, the line was never constructed.

Apart from interruption during the First World War, services from Brighton to Kemp Town continued until 2nd January 1933, a date which coincided with the last steam trains from London to Brighton. Tram and bus competition locally had eventually forced closure. The station remained open until June 1971 for use as a goods depot but after that date all track was dismantled. The once spectacular 14-arch viaduct across Lewes Road and the shorter Hartington Road viaduct were subsequently demolished and two well-known Brighton landmarks had gone.

In Hartington Road stands a fitting reminder of the earlier railway days with a home for elderly residents called Old Viaduct Court. Many of the folk can of course well remember the steam trains puffing their way across the viaducts and perhaps their memories are rekindled by a supermarket just off Lewes Road. The building has an inbuilt archway effect along the side.

In 1974 Kemp Town station site became Freshfield Industrial Estate. At the northern end where trains once emerged from chalk cliffs, the tunnel, available for use as an air raid shelter from 1941 to 1944, found use as a mushroom farm.

Volk's 'Daddy Long-Legs' Tramway

'Pioneer', affectionately known as 'Daddy Long-Legs', a sea-going railway photographed off Brighton front, c1899. It began in 1896 and proved quite a sensation but it lasted only a few years. (Pamlin Prints)

In 1896 an unusual idea came from Magnus Volk who was already well known for his electric railway along the sea front. An electric tramway was built to travel over 60 yards from the shore between a landing platform at Banjo Groyne and a light steel pier 100 yards long at Rottingdean. Two sets of double track of 2 ft 8½ inch gauge, set 18 ft apart, were built and standards erected to support the overhead wires. At high tide the contraption, affectionately known as 'Daddy Long-Legs', was seen to be travelling through the water!

The sea-going car, known as *Pioneer*, stood high on 4 legs each 23 ft long. There was seating inside and also above on an open top. In the interior there was an upholstered 'knifeboard' seat along the centre with further seating provided at each end. Between the centre seat backs, plants and flowers were provided and many of the windows, particularly on the seaward side, were heavily curtained.

The tram was quite a sensation in Brighton but unfortunately for the town's visitors it lasted only until 1901. It opened on 28th November 1896 but disaster struck within only a few days with a bad storm on the night of 4th December. Damage was so bad that the line closed and plans to build a second car were abandoned because of high repair costs. *Pioneer* was roped to the Rottingdean pier. Despite this she broke away, ran some distance down the line and capsized. Reopening was not until July 1897 after many alterations had been made but the company never really survived its losses and services finally ceased in 1901.

Pioneer survived until at least 1909 roped to an intermediate landing stage at Ovingdean Gap but was finally dismantled along with the piers and track shortly afterwards. The metal went to Germany and no doubt returned to Britain during the First World War in a slightly different form! Today it is still just possible at low tide to see the seaweed-covered concrete blocks which once supported the tracks.

12
More Lines Meet Their End

Kent & East Sussex Railway
Rye Harbour
Rye & Camber Tramway
Crowhurst to Bexhill

0-6-0T locomotive 32678 with passenger coach arrives at Tenterden from Robertsbridge in the 1950s. The line closed to passengers in 1954, remaining open for freight until 1961. (John H. Meredith)

Kent & East Sussex Railway

The Kent & East Sussex Railway (KESR) with its classic rural tracks of sharp curves and steep gradients first came to the drawing board in the 1850s. Yet it was a campaign by angry locals that eventually made the line a reality. Numerous proposals had been put forward but it was a line from Robertsbridge to Headcorn that finally won the day. It was known initially as The Rother Valley (Light) Railway, approved by a Light Railway Order in 1896, incorporated to build a line from Robertsbridge on the SER Tonbridge-Hastings line to Tenterden. In 1903 a Light Railway Order was obtained for an extension from Tenterden to the SER Tonbridge-Ashford line at Headcorn. A further Order in 1904 altered the name of the company to the Kent & East Sussex Light Railway (KESR). The line was built under the direction of Colonel Holman F. Stephens.

Trains from Robertsbridge to Rolvenden commenced in 1900 and extended to Tenterden in 1903. Headcorn was reached another two years later. The line expected a good income with monthly markets held at Robertsbridge, two large flour mills served by special sidings and a thriving farming community

Tenterden Town station looking eastwards in June 1948. After complete closure in 1961 the branch partly re-opened in 1974 as a preserved line between Tenterden and Rolvenden. (John H. Meredith)

Robertsbridge station, c1938, where passengers changed for the KESR trains. Ex-SECR class P 0-6-0T locomotive 1556 has arrived from Headcorn with a selection of mixed coaches. (S.C.Townroe/R.K. Blencowe)

Bodiam station photographed before closure of the branch. Today a preserved railway reaches Bodiam, famous for its nearby castle. (R.K. Blencowe)

along the route. Hop growing was also a strong feature of the area.

Another attraction was Bodiam Castle which could sometimes expect as many as 600 visitors in one day. Previously people had arrived in horse-pulled brakes from St Leonards and Hastings at a cost of 4s 6d each but now the railway could offer the journey at half the price.

The KESR from Robertsbridge followed the Rother Valley and the line had to be built high enough to avoid flooding. Even so in 1916 the track was not only under water but it moved due to pressure. The situation was discovered when the engine pulling the first train of the day was derailed. It came to rest on its side against a fortunately placed willow tree.

By the late 1930s the line was falling into decline. The locomotive stock became very run down and Southern Railway tank locomotives were frequently borrowed. Use was made of petrol-engined railcars, one having been purchased from Shefflex, similar to one used on the Selsey Tramway.

KESR locomotive AIX Terrier 0-6-0T no 3 (later BR no 32670) photographed at Robertsbridge on 19th June 1948. It was built in 1872. (John H. Meredith)

A well-worn sign reminds passers-by of the Rother Valley Railway (KESR from 1904). This picture was taken at Rolvenden in June 1948. (John H. Meredith)

The Second World War helped the KESR to regain some of its importance becoming a secondary route towards the coast when main lines were hit by German bombs. In January 1948 the KESR became part of British Railways Southern Region and an inspection of the track and rolling stock revealed many deficiencies. Of the nine coaches only two were retained and many trucks were scrapped. Despite this the KESR line survived a further five years.

The last passenger train ran on a cold and wet day in January 1954 but the Robertsbridge to Tenterden stretch remained open for goods traffic until 1961. During this time a number of hop pickers' trains used the line and in addition four specials were organised, one by the Branch Line Society, another by the Ramblers' Association and two more by the Locomotive Club of Great Britain.

This was not to be the end however. The Kent & East Sussex

Kent & East Sussex trains reached Bodiam station in April 2000. Diesel railcars await return to Tenterden. (Author)

Railway Preservation Society (later called the Tenterden Railway Company Limited) came into being and in 1974 a section of the track was reopened. Initially trains ran from Tenterden Town to Rolvenden only. Northiam station was reached in June 1990 and in April 2000 trains reached Bodiam, 100 years to the day since trains first steamed along the track. The event was celebrated with Sir Alastair Morton, Strategic Rail Authority Chairman, officiating at a grand ceremony to mark the completion of the 'Millennium Extension'.

Rye Harbour

Two further areas remain to be mentioned and one of these is at Rye. The town was initially served by the SER line from Hastings to Ashford which opened in 1851 and three years later in March 1854 a line for goods only was opened from Rye to Rye Harbour.

The branch crossed the A259 Rye to Winchelsea road and then the River Brede at OS ref 920198. To the south a level crossing existed at OS 935193 and the terminus can be located at Rye Harbour village on the bank of the River Rother just above the slipway. The line served a nearby oil firm and a chemical works with private sidings and also carried flints brought from Dungeness. The short branch closed in 1962 when the track was removed.

Rye & Camber Tramway

A useful passenger service was provided by a 3 ft narrow gauge line which ran from Rye to Camber Sands. When it opened in 1895 its intention was to serve Camber Golf Links only but it proved immediately successful to holidaymakers and in its first

The Rye & Camber Tramway began in 1895 with steam traction to cross the marshes from Rye to Camber Golf Links. In 1925 it converted to petrol traction, the locomotive being described locally as 'a king-sized lawn-mower'. (Lens of Sutton)

The Rye & Camber Tramway was successful in its early days. In the first 6 months it carried 18,000 passengers. The tramway extended to Camber Sands in July 1908. (Lens of Sutton)

six months sold 18,000 tickets. In 1908 the line was extended to Camber Sands.

Initially drawn by steam, the tramway partially converted to petrol in 1925 when the company purchased a motor which at the time was described as looking more like 'a king-sized lawnmower'. One of its steam locomotives was sold the following year but the second (and only other) locomotive survived until 1937. But receipts were falling and when war broke out in 1939, the line was closed. Part of the track was converted to road by the army to give access to the east side of Rye Harbour and to a complex of army nissen huts.

The track was finally lifted in 1945 but despite this parts of the line can still be traced. The Rye terminus can be found on the south side of the A259 Rye to New Romney road across a bridge over the River Rother. At Rye Harbour a corrugated iron building which was once Golf Links station survived for many years as the office of a boat hire company. At Camber Sands the terminus can be located 400 yards south of Camber Road among the sand dunes at OS 952188.

Crowhurst to Bexhill

Finally a link between Crowhurst and Bexhill West is worthy of mention. This was a 4½ mile branch from the SER Tonbridge to Hastings line across a broad valley and down to the coastal suburbs of Bexhill. The Crowhurst, Sidley & Bexhill Railway company was incorporated in 1897 and it received approval to proceed in the same year. The company had connections with the SER and the branch proposed gave a through route from the Capital to Bexhill that was quicker on SER lines than on those of the LBSCR. Added to this Bexhill was anxious to promote itself as a leading seaside resort and one of the measures it took to increase popularity was to permit mixed bathing!

Crowhurst on the main line to Hastings where passengers could change for Sidley and Bexhill West. This was an SER branch built to compete with LBSCR trains to Bexhill. (Lens of Sutton)

Sidley station building, c1900, before the motor age. The short branch to Bexhill West included a magnificent 17-arch viaduct over the Crowhurst Valley but after closure of the branch in 1964 it was blown up. (Lens of Sutton)

Sidley station with its deserted platforms not long before closure. The bridge beyond the station carries the A269. After closure the station was demolished to become a private garage. (Lens of Sutton)

A branch to Bexhill was therefore desirable and construction was completed by June 1902. Earlier a line had been proposed by the LBSCR from Rotherfield on the Cuckoo Line to Bexhill but in the face of effective competition this idea fell away. The Crowhurst branch was not unexpectedly absorbed by the SER in 1905.

The line was double-track and included a magnificent 17-arch viaduct across the Crowhurst Valley which had a maximum height of 70 ft. Thereafter the track descended to Sidley, the only intermediate station. Bexhill West (originally called Bexhill) was a large station with a long two-faced platform and room for extension. There was a large goods depot and there were extensive sidings.

Initially the SER carried more passengers, the route being nearly ten miles shorter from London than via the LBSCR line through Eastbourne. By 1925 there were 18 weekday departures from Crowhurst but electrification of the LBSCR (by now SR) line in 1935 took the traffic back and the Crowhurst line declined.

Despite the use of push-pull trains and, later, diesel-electric units, the branch line finally closed on 15th June 1964. Sadly the 17-arch viaduct has long since been blown up and Sidley station, south of an overbridge on the A269, became a private garage. After closure Bexhill West station was demolished and the site became an antique auction room as well as a pub / disco.

Conclusion

The decline of many Sussex lines came during the 1920s. Buses were on the increase, providing a more flexible service than the trains. In addition, road haulage was growing. Early casualties were the Selsey Tramway and the Dyke Railway which could hardly survive with faster and more frequent bus services running almost parallel to the tracks. The Rye & Camber Tramway also failed because of bus competition although when the Second World War came, the line was handed over to the Admiralty. During hostilities it was put to good use but when returned to its original owners in 1945, it was found to be unusable.

Another factor contributing to the decline of the railways was the elimination of competition between private companies brought about by 'grouping' in 1923. This had the effect of merging more than 100 companies throughout Great Britain into four main companies: LNER (London & North Eastern Railway), LMS (London, Midland & Scottish Railway), GWR (Great Western Railway) and SR (Southern Railway).

Meantime changes were taking place which were to materially affect the railways and their future. With paid holidays and rising living standards becoming accepted conditions of employment, people were willing to live further from their place of work. Electricity was more freely available and with the coalfields of the North no longer vital to industry, people were migrating southwards. The Home Counties became a popular area bringing with it the need to provide extensive suburban rail services between the Capital and the surrounding districts.

It was in this climate that the Southern Railway developed its electric services. An AC overhead system had already been inherited from its predecessors, the LBSCR, providing services as far south as Coulsdon North and Sutton. In 1926 the present DC system was adopted and by 1928 'third rail electrics' were installed along the old SER lines to Caterham and Tattenham Corner. Eventually, threatened by effective coach and motorcar competition between London and Brighton, electric trains were provided to the coast. The last scheduled steam train left Victoria for Brighton on 31st December 1932 and electric services began the next day.

Benefits were immediate. Traffic increased and by 1933 passenger numbers had increased by 127%. Track layouts were changed to accommodate the new trains, signalling systems were modernised and platforms reorganised. Timetables were altered to give more frequent services at regular intervals, considerably increased during peak travel periods. During the next few years, electrification extended rapidly throughout much of the network.

The war effectively wrecked the finances of the railways which were to be saved by nationalisation in 1948. But with Government subsidies involved it was inevitable that 'rationalisation' processes would follow. Progress to commence capital investment programmes was slow due to material shortages. In addition, integration with other forms of transport, a declared aim of nationalisation, made little headway.

Despite optimistic plans for redevelopment, freight traffic was on the decline and the railways were becoming more dependent on passenger traffic. By the early 1960s the Government's attitude had hardened. In the Transport Act of 1962, it was clear that commercial viability was considered a more important factor than providing a service to the public. In 1963 the Minister of Transport appointed the Stedeford Group to look at the future of the railways. The findings were not published but one of its members was Dr Richard Beeching (later Lord Beeching), a name that was to become very well known in the years to come.

In March 1963 proposals were made in a report which became popularly known as the 'Beeching Plan'. The idea was to keep lines considered suitable to rail traffic and give up the remainder. When the closures came over the next few years, some lines went quietly but others went only after a struggle. For numerous towns and villages, the disappearance of trains caused considerable social upheaval and many suffered as a result.

When rail privatisation came in the mid-1990s rail travellers were told it would give them an exciting future. Yet press reports continually indicate that 'complaints about late, cancelled and overcrowded trains have soared. Figures point to an alarming deterioration in services'. The need for continuing track repairs and ever increasing rail fares more than endorse this view. The Channel Tunnel, although providing rapid links with European capitals, still has to provide high-speed trains in the UK and the tunnel has yet to prove itself financially.

During research in the region, the author was appalled at the very high density of traffic on roads in the Sussex area, private and commercial. What plans are in hand to avoid total congestion of our highways within just a few years while railway lines have been axed or are inefficiently used? There is talk, but only talk, of 'piggyback trucks' by rail, a feature popular in many European countries. Container traffic could also surely be maximised.

It is encouraging that plans are being considered to electrify the Uckfield branch as well as the line from Hastings to Ashford. Despite these ideas, for the nostalgic it is sad indeed that such a large area of railways in the Weald has been so completely wiped out. Surely the early pioneers of the 19th century would turn in their graves at the thought of today's railway system.

Opening and Final Closure Dates of Lines to Regular Passenger Traffic

Line	Opened	Final Closure
Polegate to Hailsham	1849	1968
Three Bridges to East Grinstead	1855	1967
Lewes to Uckfield	1858	1969(1)
Pulborough to Petworth	1859	1955
Shoreham to Christ's Hospital	1861	1966
Midhurst to Petersfield	1864	1955
Christ's Hospital to Guildford	1865	1965
Petworth to Midhurst	1866	1955
East Grinstead to Groombridge	1866	1967
Groombridge to Tunbridge Wells	1866	1985(2)
Kemp Town Branch Line	1869	1933
Hellingly to Hellingly Mental Hospital	1880	1931
Hailsham to Eridge	1880	1965
Midhurst to Chichester	1881	1935
Lewes to East Grinstead	1882	1958(3)(4)
Horsted Keynes to Haywards Heath	1883	1963
The Dyke Railway	1887	1939
Rye to Camber Golf Links	1895	1939
Selsey Tramway (Chichester to Selsey)	1897	1935
Selsey Beach Extension	1898	1904
Robertsbridge to Rolvenden	1900	1954(5)
Crowhurst to Bexhill West	1902	1964

Rolvenden to Tenterden Town	1903	1954(5)
Tenterden Town to Headcorn	1905	1954
Camber Golf Links to Camber Sands	1908	1939

(1) Lavender Line opened at Isfield 1983
(2) Spa Valley Line opened 1996
(3) Limited service from August 1956 to March 1958
(4) Section reopened by Bluebell Railway Preservation Society May 1960
(5) Section reopened by Tenterden Railway Company Limited in 1974

Bibliography

In compiling *Lost Railways of Sussex*, I have referred to numerous sources, many now out of print, which include the following and which can be recommended for further reading:

Course, Edwin *The Railways of Southern England* and *Independent and Light Railways* (B. T. Batsford Ltd)

Dendy Marshall, C. F. (revised by R.W. Kidner) *History of the Southern Railway* (Ian Allan Ltd)

Gray, Adrian *The Railways of Mid-Sussex* and *The London to Brighton Line* (Oakwood Press)

Hadfield, Charles *The Canals of South and South East England* (David & Charles)

Howard Turner, J. T. *The London, Brighton & South Coast Railway: 1 Origins and Formations, 2 Establishment and Growth, 3 Completion and Maturity* (B. T. Batsford Ltd)

White, H. P. *Forgotten Railways: South East England* and *A Regional History of the Railways of Great Britain, Vol 2: Southern England* (David & Charles)

Index